Making a Killing

Making a Killing

The Deadly Implications of the Counterfeit Drug Trade

Roger Bate

DISCARD

The AEI Press

Publisher for the American Enterprise Institute

WASHINGTON, D.C.

Distributed to the Trade by National Book Network, 15200 NBN Way, Blue Ridge Summit, PA 17214. To order call toll free 1-800-462-6420 or 1-717-794-3800. For all other inquiries please contact the AEI Press, 1150 Seventeenth Street, N.W., Washington, D.C. 20036 or call 1-800-862-5801.

Library of Congress Cataloging-in-Publication Data

Bate, Roger.
Making a killing : the deadly implications of the counterfeit drug trade / Roger Bate.
    p. ; cm.

Includes bibliographical references.
   ISBN-13: 978-0-8447-4264-9
   ISBN-10: 0-8447-4264-3

  1. Drug traffic. 2. Drug adulteration. 3. Pharmaceutical industry—Corrupt practices. 4. Product counterfeiting. I. Title.
  [DNLM: 1. Drug Industry. 2. Fraud. 3. Drug and Narcotic Control. QV 773 B328m 2008]

     HV8079.N3B38 2008
     364.1'42—dc22

                                      2008015497

12 11 10 09 08   1 2 3 4 5

Printed in the United States of America

Contents

LIST OF ILLUSTRATIONS   vii

ACKNOWLEDGMENTS   ix

INTRODUCTION: THE SECOND-OLDEST PROFESSION   1
     Definitions and Scope   4

1. COUNTERFEITING TODAY   8
     Counterfeit Drugs in Industrialized Economies   8
       Compromised Supply Chains   8
       Internet Sales   9
       Drugs Targeted   12
     Counterfeit Drugs in Developing Countries   14
       Africa   17
       Latin America   20
       Russia   21
       Asia   23

2. HOW AND WHY DOES COUNTERFEITING OCCUR?   25
     Incentives to Counterfeit   25
     Corruption within Countries   27
     Complex Supply Chains Encourage Fakes   28
       Developed Countries   28
       Developing Countries   33
     Counterfeiting, Organized Crime, and Terrorism   35
     Conclusion   37

3. STOPPING THE FAKERS   39
     At the International Level   39
     At the National Level   41

Developed Countries   41
  Japan   *41*
  United States   *43*
  European Union   *44*
Developing Countries   45
  Africa   *46*
  Latin America   *50*
  Russia   *51*
  Asia   *52*
Unilateral Private Action   57
  Independent Organizations   57
  Pharmaceutical Companies   59
  Pharmacists   60

4. POLICY RECOMMENDATIONS   61
At the International Level   *61*
  Donor Agencies   61
  Aid Agencies   62
At the National Level   *63*
  Developing Countries   63
  Western Countries   66
  Public and Private Actors   67
  Governments   68
  Policymakers   71
At the Business Level   *72*
  Pharmaceutical Companies   72
At the Individual Level   *72*
  Public-Private Cooperation   73

CONCLUSION   75

NOTES   77

ABOUT THE AUTHOR   105

List of Illustrations

FIGURES

I-1   Five Shilling Bill of Credit, "To Counterfeit Is Death"   2
1-1   Reports of Counterfeit Drugs by Therapeutic Class
         Received by WHO, 1999–2002   13
1-2   Authentic v. Counterfeit Voveran (Pain Medication)
         Pills   17
1-3   Percent Failure of Chloroquine (Antimalarial Drug)
         in African Countries   18
2-1   Drug Supply Chains   31
3-1   Counterfeit Drug Cases Opened by the FDA,
         1997–2006   43

TABLE

1-1   Prevalence of Counterfeit Drugs in the West and
         the Developing World   14

Acknowledgments

I'd like to thank my colleagues Jack Calfee and Lorraine Mooney and Andrew Jackson, chief of corporate security for Novartis, for their useful comments on this book. I'd also particularly like to note the excellent research of my current assistant Karen Porter and former AEI researchers Evan Daar and Kathryn Boateng, who worked with me on this project in 2007. In addition, the editorial staff at AEI have provided valuable input and critiquing of all drafts of the manuscript. Other experts, who'd prefer to remain anonymous, have reviewed parts of the manuscript. I thank them for their help; they know who they are.

Introduction

The Second-Oldest Profession

As long as people have been in the business of inventing, others have been in the business of faking their inventions. Counterfeiting has played a role in padding business profits, waging war, defrauding governments, and undermining currencies. Today, fake medicines are harming health and impeding pharmaceutical innovation.

Documents from the second century BC tell the story of a Gallic winemaker who tried to pass off cheap local wine as a much finer Italian vintage. Most wines were transported in clay jars, and merchants would make an imprint on the stopper to indicate the wine's origin and quality. The unschooled Gaul made his own stopper to resemble those of more established wines. But his plan had one major flaw: He could neither read nor write. Instead of marking the name of a recognized Italian winemaker, he settled for a few indecipherable characters. The merchant's clay stopper now sits in a glass case at the Union des Fabricants's Museum of Counterfeiting in Paris, an example of one of the world's first knockoffs.[1]

A faker will exploit every possibility. In 1690, Thomas and Anne Rogers were executed in England for clipping the edges off of forty pieces of silver to make new coins from them. Punishment for counterfeiting was severe. Thomas was hanged, drawn, and quartered; Anne was burned alive.[2]

In the United States in the early eighteenth century, lax control of the money supply led many people to attempt to counterfeit money. Mary Peck Butterworth, a homemaker in rural Massachusetts, used a hot iron, a piece of cloth, and a quill pen to create counterfeit versions of colonial currency.[3] Later, during the Revolutionary War,

1

FIGURE I-1
"TWENTY SHILLING NOTE, TO COUNTERFEIT IS DEATH"

SOURCE: Courtesy of the Eric P. Newman Numismatic Education Society.
NOTE: "To Counterfeit Is Death," Pennsylvania Five Shilling Bill of Credit, printed by
Franklin and Hall, Philadelphia, 1758.

the British used counterfeiting strategically. British soldiers flooded
the American market with so much counterfeit cash that the conti-
nental became worthless—the origin of the phrase "not worth a con-
tinental."[4] The most famous American printer, Benjamin Franklin,
was acutely aware of the damage counterfeiters could do. He printed
detailed pictures of leaves on his currency that were too complex to
fake easily. He also printed the slogan "To Counterfeit Is Death" on
each of his notes—an expression more of frustration than fact.[5]

Fake and substandard pharmaceuticals have posed a threat to
people's health for centuries.[6] As technological capabilities advanced
through the nineteenth and twentieth centuries, counterfeiters
turned to faking whatever goods were most profitable or most easily procured and distributed without detection: cigarettes, jewelry,
digital media—and medicine.[7] Modern efforts to combat such counterfeiting have focused on establishing universal standards for
drug quality and empowering watchdog agencies.

Baseline standards for medicines were established in the United States by U.S. Pharmacopeia (USP) in 1820. Societies of medicine from all twenty-three states were invited to send delegates to meet and discuss drug quality issues. The USP created a system of drug production standards and a system of quality control, as well as formulae (agreed-upon sets of symbols showing the chemical composition of drugs), and a national formulary (an updated list of medicines and related information representing the latest clinical judgments of physicians, pharmacists, and other experts). Only 217 drugs that met the criteria of "most fully established and best understood" were included on this list.[8]

In 1848, Congress passed the Drug Importation Act, which required U.S. customs officials to inspect and analyze imported drugs for "quality, purity, and fitness for medical purposes."[9] Since then, the USP and other interested parties—including drug manufacturers, pharmacists, patient groups, and the federal government—have attempted to protect patients from adulterated medicines.

Despite such efforts, however, counterfeit drugs managed to breach the system, and they continue to do so today, both in the United States and other countries. In 1937, more than a hundred Americans were killed when they took medicine containing the dangerous solvent diethylene glycol. In 2006, more than a hundred children in Panama died after ingesting the very same solvent mixed into cough syrup. The solvent had been falsely identified and exported as glycerin, a sweet-tasting syrup that is a common ingredient in medicine, and, in the latter case, was traced to a Chinese chemical company.[10]

Because counterfeiting represents such an easy and potentially lucrative opportunity for commercial profit, and because it spans industries as diverse as wine, electronics, and medicine, it likely will never be eradicated. Still, if its characteristics are identified and its real effects understood, its impact may be mitigated substantially. Nowhere is this more evident—and important—than in the battle against the counterfeiting of lifesaving pharmaceuticals, a trade with dangerous implications for public health.

Definitions and Scope

Fake drugs and active pharmaceutical ingredients most often originate in emerging industrial economies—especially India—before
entering the global market. Trafficking in counterfeit drugs has
become one of the fastest-growing criminal businesses. Improved
technological capabilities have enabled counterfeiters to produce
packaging that looks good enough to fool legitimate wholesalers and
retailers. The Internet offers fakers direct access to people seeking
too-cheap-to-be-true therapeutics, or to those embarrassed to get
prescriptions for "lifestyle drugs," such as those that treat impotence.

Although rich countries are the most lucrative potential markets
for fakes, they also have the best protections against them. Most
developed economies have laws and enforcement procedures to combat counterfeiting and other fraudulent activities. Many have national
drug regulatory authorities and organized chains of supply, with
highly educated pharmacists. The World Health Organization (WHO)
has estimated that fake drugs represent less than 1 percent of market
value in these economies.[11]

Much easier for counterfeiters is pushing high volumes of fake
painkillers, antibiotics, and antiprotozoals (such as antimalarial
drugs) into unregulated markets—that is, the poorest countries,
which are also the most vulnerable to infectious diseases. WHO estimates that many countries in Africa, Latin America, and parts of
Asia have areas where more than 30 percent of the medicines on
sale may be counterfeit; in many of the former Soviet republics, the
proportion is 20 percent.[12]

The most obvious risk of unproven drugs is to a patient's health.
Taking a drug with an incorrect formula of active ingredients—or
with the wrong ingredients—can have serious adverse health effects.
Taking a drug without *any* active ingredients, a common counterfeiting instance, can lead a sick patient who *thinks* he or she is being
treated to forgo real treatment until it is too late. Taking a drug with
only *some* of the correct ingredients can cause a patient to develop
resistance to that particular drug, making it harder for the patient to
be treated with effective medicines later on. This has effects at the

population level as well, as resistance increases far more
would otherwise be the case, making specific legitimate d
entire classes of drugs useless—even for those who have
ously taken counterfeit or substandard drugs.

WHO defines a counterfeit drug as one that is

> deliberately and fraudulently mislabeled with respect to
> identity and/or source. Counterfeiting can apply to both
> branded and generic products and counterfeit products may
> include products with the correct ingredients or with the
> wrong ingredients, without active ingredients, with insuffi-
> cient active ingredients or with fake packaging.[13]

Counterfeiting can also include bulk ingredients made to produce drugs.

Unfortunately, there is no consensus about this definition.
Countries issuing their own regulations against counterfeiting
have their own definitions, making information exchange among
them difficult and hindering the development of global anti-fake
strategies. Some countries do not enforce their regulations, and
others do not even have any regulations to enforce.

According to WHO, only about 20 percent of member states
have well-developed regulations against counterfeiting. Another
50 percent operate at varying levels of regulation and capacity, and
30 percent have weak regulation or none at all. Despite its policy of
confidentiality regarding reports of counterfeiting, fewer than 5 percent of member states actually divulge such information to WHO.
The reports that are made are not validated, and some reports do
not distinguish between counterfeit and substandard drugs.[14]

The distinction between counterfeit and substandard drugs is
an important one. WHO defines a substandard drug as one which
does not *intentionally* have incorrect packaging, but may have the
incorrect quantity or ratio of ingredients. Unlike counterfeits, substandard drugs do not represent deliberate attempts by miscreants
to dupe consumers, but rather are the result of a legal manufacturer's shoddy production. This category also includes drugs that are

produced in compliance with WHO's good manufacturing practice (GMP) guidelines[15] and pass quality inspections on the factory floor, but are rendered ineffective by poor transit or inadequate storage along the supply chain. This may be the result of either ignorance or carelessness. Many pharmaceuticals, including several vital antiretroviral (ARV), antibiotic, cancer, and antiprotozoal drugs, require specific storage temperatures to ensure their effectiveness. A 1997 study in a Zambian hospital, for example, found that several HIV antibody assays no longer worked effectively because they had been improperly stored or were past their expiration date.[16] In the developing world, distributors and local pharmacies may not have the ability—or incentives—to adhere to proper standards, especially for drugs requiring refrigeration during transit and storage.

Substandard drugs are rare in the countries of the European Union (EU) and in the United States, since both have comparatively rigorous customs controls, import-quality regulations, internal quality controls on wholesalers, and, most importantly, pharmacies with reputations to maintain. In the developing world, however, such drugs are rife.[17] Weak regulation in these countries[18] is also increasingly allowing substandard and counterfeit drugs to infiltrate the supply chains of the developed world.

Although the proliferation of substandard drugs is a major policy issue worthy of attention, this book focuses primarily on counterfeit drugs, that is, drugs willfully mislabeled as to identity or source. Nonetheless, differences in definition aside, it is important to note that the distinction between counterfeit drugs (intentionally deficient) and substandard ones (unintentionally deficient) can be tenuous in practice. This is particularly the case when one includes state actors in the analysis. As discussed above, many developing-world governments lack effective regulation to monitor drug production in their countries. Nevertheless, prompted by political and economic incentives, they continue to permit and even push for local production enterprises that may or may not have the technical capabilities to ensure compliance with GMP and ongoing quality checks.[19] In Thailand, for example, the government promoted the distribution of a cheap—but substandard—ARV, GPO-Vir, that was produced by the state-run Government Pharmaceutical Organization. By the time the factory was forced to shut down in 2007 (with its reopening contingent on improvements in its production facilities), resistance among users of GPO-Vir had already reached a rate of perhaps 50 percent.[20] By pursuing a local production project with little heed for quality control, Thai officials intentionally enabled the production of substandard products—second-degree counterfeiting, if you will.

In chapter 1, I will outline the extent of the counterfeiting problem around the world today, from Internet pharmacies in the United States to Russia's "gray" market, from Africa's unscrupulous street vendors to China's fake export industry. Chapter 2 explores dynamics of the counterfeit-drug trade, such as fakers' economic incentives, complex supply chains, unwieldy tariffs, and the involvement of organized crime in the fake-drug trade. Signs of progress in the fight against counterfeit drugs are described in chapter 3, from country-level efforts around the world to international and corporate initiatives. Finally, chapter 4 offers several concrete and realistic policy recommendations that can help make counterfeiting sufficiently unprofitable as to render it impotent.

1

Counterfeiting Today

Counterfeit pharmaceuticals are a problem all around the world, and they affect people of various income levels. Although their impact is concentrated among the poor in the developing world, their distribution is by no means exclusive to them. This chapter sketches the dynamics of drug counterfeiting, from Canadian Internet pharmacies and the European supply chain to New Delhi street vendors and illicit nightshifts at Russian drug factories.

Counterfeit Drugs in Industrialized Economies

The value of the counterfeit drug market in the United States has been estimated at $39 billion annually.[1] Such a figure is, at best, a guess. The Pharmaceutical Security Institute (PSI), a nonprofit partnership among pharmaceutical companies founded in 1996 in part to determine the extent of the counterfeit drug problem, reported that the value of *seized* counterfeit and diverted drugs in the United States was only $200 million in 2003.[2] But the total number of counterfeit drugs undetected is likely to be much higher. Statistics are no better in the EU, where data on seizures provide the only accurate figures available. For example, the European Commission announced that its customs department had seized 2.7 million fake tablets in 2006, most of them originating in India.[3]

Counterfeit drugs make their way into developed countries in several ways.

Compromised Supply Chains. In recent years, counterfeit and substandard drugs have turned up in the supply chains of developed countries—the legitimate, legally recognized chains from drug producers to consumers that include wholesalers and retail outlets. In some instances, these fakes (which may also include medical products, particularly where the market is large) have found their way into private U.S. pharmaceutical supply chains, which consist of the pharmaceutical company, private wholesalers, and private pharmacies. In 2003, for example, fake Lipitor—a cholesterol-lowering drug—was discovered in neighborhood pharmacies in the United States.[4] At some point along this supply chain, a counterfeiter passes his or her drugs off as legitimate, often posing as a wholesaler acting as a middleman between the manufacturer and the distributor. In one case, a Canadian wholesaler who sold counterfeit OneTouch diabetes test strips to U.S. pharmacies claimed to have bought the faulty strips from a Chinese distributor of LifeScan products.[5]

Some distributors are complicit in the counterfeiting scheme, knowingly purchasing cheap fakes and selling them to consumers at the price of legitimate goods, making a killing. In May 2006 U.S. officials discovered a package from China containing several thousand counterfeit Viagra and Cialis pills, which a Texas pharmacist had planned to sell.[6]

In the United Kingdom, fake versions of an obesity drug and an impotence drug were discovered within days of each other in 2004. Health officials said it was the first time counterfeit drugs had breached the British supply chain since 1994,[7] but the trend is up, with nine known cases of fake drugs reaching patients in the past three years.[8] A chance inspection by British customs officers in 2007 uncovered a large operation in which fake Viagra was being shipped to factories in Britain, where it was repackaged and sold online to customers in thirty-five countries, including Great Britain, the United States, and Canada.[9]

Internet Sales. Hundreds of online "pharmacies" advertise themselves as cheap, fast alternatives to typical drugstores in developed countries. For Americans facing the highest pharmaceutical prices in the world, these websites can be an enormous temptation. In some ways, the Internet has improved the pharmaceutical market, with increased patient access and economic efficiency, but it is also a major source of counterfeit distribution. A 2004 study by the U.S. Government Accountability Office (GAO) found that four out of twenty-one medicines ordered from websites outside the United States or Canada were counterfeit.[10]

An online pharmacy that hides its physical address is more likely to sell counterfeits instead of the legitimate branded drugs it offers. The source of the drug and its chain of custody remain largely mysterious to the consumer. One website claimed to distribute Januvaria, one of Merck's flagship diabetes medicines. It proudly displayed Merck's logo and even a photograph of its vice president for public affairs. But Merck had no knowledge of the Internet entity; it was a fake.[11] As a warning to U.S. consumers, the Food and Drug Administration (FDA) recently listed on its website online pharmacies that may sell counterfeit medicines in the United States, most of the time without prescriptions.[12] In February 2004, the FDA shut down the website www.rxpharmacy.ws, whose domain name is registered in Samoa, for selling counterfeit contraceptive patches to women in the United States.[13] The patches contained no active ingredients and were packaged in simple, resealable zipper plastic bags.[14]

Many online pharmacies that advertise to U.S. consumers claim to be based in Canada, where government-imposed ceilings control the price of drugs, and many Americans have flocked to these pharmacies to fill their prescriptions. But many of these "Canadian pharmacies" are really just web addresses for front companies that ship counterfeit drugs. In July 2004, FDA officials purchased so-called "generic" versions of Lipitor, Viagra, and Ambien from a website advertising "Canadian generics." But none of these drugs are produced in generic form; all drugs the FDA purchased were counterfeit.[15] These "ghost" drugs may be particularly easy to counterfeit: if the consumer does not know that the generic version of the drug does not exist, the packaging used does not have to replicate anything. As long as it appears to be professional, the consumer may never know. In the case of the "Canadian generics," the FDA discovered upon further investigation that the registered owners of the website were not in Canada, but in China and Belize.[16]

In December 2005, the FDA tested a batch of imported drugs from different Canadian pharmacies and discovered that many drugs had been produced in other countries and were counterfeit.[17] Other shipments of so-called Canadian drugs have been traced to places as diverse as Panama, Mauritius, and the Bahamas.[18] Once such an order is filled, it is boxed and shipped to an intermediary, often in the United Kingdom. From there, the package is mailed to the U.S. consumer without ever passing through Canada. The FDA estimates that as many as 85 percent of drugs promoted as Canadian actually come from other countries around the world, including India, Costa Rica, and Vanuatu.[19]

Even drugs that actually come from Canada carry no safety guarantee. Mediplan Prescription Plus Pharmacy is one of the leading Canadian Internet pharmacies that ships to the United States. The FDA warned consumers in 2006 that versions of Lipitor, Crestor, Celebrex, and seven other types of drugs shipped from Mediplan into the United States were counterfeit.[20] Some of the drugs tested did not even originate in Canada, and many did not contain the proper ratios of active ingredients.[21]

Online pharmacies that peddle counterfeit drugs are based in the United States, too. In October 2006, the U.S. Drug Enforcement Agency (DEA) arrested eleven employees of a Georgia-based drug manufacturer that was selling fake pharmaceuticals over the Internet to U.S. consumers. The group's revenues topped $19 million.[22] In 2006, the Federal Bureau of Investigation (FBI) investigated a Philadelphia-based Internet pharmacy that smuggled an estimated 2.5 million dosage units of drugs into the United States from India, including Vicodin, anabolic steroids, and amphetamines.[23]

The anonymity of the Internet is attractive to fakers and customers alike—to the latter for buying drugs associated with social stigmas. In 2007, for example, in the largest counterfeit-drug bust in the United States to date, British customs officials unearthed a conspiracy to supply millions of pounds worth of counterfeit Viagra and drugs used to treat male hair loss. According to BBC correspondent Jon Brain, the conspirators assumed that customers would be too bashful about their use of such "lifestyle" drugs to report problems to the authorities. When sentencing one of the conspirators, Judge Nicholas Price noted that consumers were "easy prey, often too embarrassed to seek help from their doctors."[24]

Drugs Targeted. For the most part, counterfeiters appear to target certain markets with specific drugs. In industrialized economies, evidence from confiscated fakes suggests that lifestyle drugs—typically the impotence drugs Viagra and Cialis that are often sold over the Internet—are favored. Customers buying from the Internet are unlikely to be familiar with the appearance or effects of the legitimate product, and they are less likely to complain if they are dissatisfied.

If the counterfeit problem in developed countries were limited to such lifestyle drugs, it would be an annoyance, but not a particularly grave menace to public health. Assuming it does not contain any poisonous substitutes, a counterfeit version of Viagra—while ineffective—is generally not a matter of life and death. (An argument can be made, moreover, that informed consumers who purchase drugs from suspect sources over the Internet might be considered negligent.) Increasingly, however, counterfeiters are beginning to target lifesaving therapeutic drugs distributed through traditional (non-Internet) supply chains, posing an especially insidious threat to people who desperately need the real thing.[25] Figure 1-1 illustrates the reports of counterfeit drugs by therapeutic class received by the World Health Organization between 1999 and 2002. Although it is impossible to say—given WHO's confidential reporting system—which countries reported which types of counterfeit cases, anecdotal evidence points to increased targeting of lifesaving drugs within developing *and* developed countries.

In 2003, German officials raided a pharmacy and seized two pallets of counterfeit AIDS drugs. Valued at almost €1 million ($1.45 million), the fake packaging and inserts discovered with them were said by the original manufacturer to look very realistic.[26] The United Kingdom's Medical and Healthcare Products Regulatory Agency (MHRA), which monitors medicines and medical products

FIGURE 1-1

REPORTS OF COUNTERFEIT DRUGS BY THERAPEUTIC CLASS
RECEIVED BY WHO, 1999–2002

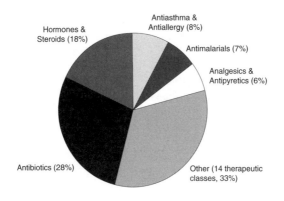

SOURCE: World Health Organization, International Medical Products Anti-Counterfeiting Taskforce (IMPACT), "Counterfeit Drugs Kill!" www.who.int/impact/resources/Impact Brochure.pdf (accessed March 17, 2008).

made or distributed in that country and has the power to prosecute counterfeiters, notes that criminals have shifted focus from using the Internet to sell small quantities of fake (predominantly lifestyle) drugs to individuals to targeting pharmaceutical wholesalers, especially those that supply public entities such as hospitals or aid organizations. By targeting wholesalers—actors further up the supply chain—counterfeiters are able to capture larger and thereby more lucrative markets more efficiently. In the summer of 2007, the MHRA issued drug alerts to health-care professionals for Plavix, a blood thinner; Zyprexa, a treatment for schizophrenia; and Casodex, a hormone treatment for prostate cancer. Because the wholesale price for a pack of twenty-eight Casodex pills in Britain is £128 ($260),[27] the profit margin available to a counterfeiter for such therapeutic drugs is huge.

TABLE 1-1

PREVALENCE OF COUNTERFEIT DRUGS IN THE WEST AND THE
DEVELOPING WORLD

OECD countries

Country/Region	Last WHO/IMPACT estimate	Other authoritative estimates
United States	<1 percent	
Europe	<1 percent	Other sources cite different figures, some as high as 10 percent.[a]
United Kingdom	<1 percent	

(*table 1-1 continued on next page*)

Counterfeit Drugs in Developing Countries

The counterfeit-drug problem is most acute in less-developed countries. Of the forty-six incidents reported to WHO between January 1999 and October 2000, twenty-eight—about 60 percent—occurred in the developing world (where reporting is rarer, which indicates that the actual number must be higher than this).[28] Country-level studies, surveys, and anecdotes tend to confirm this. One study suggests that, on average, 25 percent of the drug supply in these countries is counterfeit.[29] In Brazil, for example, over two hundred women became pregnant in 1998 after taking oral contraceptive pills made of nothing but wheat flour.[30] In Pakistan, gaps in the process of drug registration and loose enforcement have led to the proliferation of counterfeits.[31] To date, deaths from adulterated pharmaceuticals worldwide have disproportionately occurred within the world's least developed countries. Table 1-1 above illustrates the prevalence of counterfeit drugs in the developing world as compared to the West. Again, because it is especially difficult to trace the paths of drugs in the former, these estimates of fakes there are likely much too low.

(*table 1-1 continued*)

Less-developed countries

Country/Region	Last WHO/IMPACT estimate	Other authoritative estimates
Africa		
Nigeria	16 percent	
Kenya	30 percent	
Lebanon	35 percent	
Asia		
Cambodia	13 percent	
China	8 percent (over-the-counter only)	
India	10–20 percent	
Indonesia	25 percent	
Eurasia		
Russia	10 percent	A different source places the figure higher, at 12 percent.[b]
Former Soviet republics	20 percent	
Latin America		
Colombia	5 percent	
Mexico	10 percent	
Peru	15–20 percent	
Venezuela	25 percent	

SOURCES: World Health Organization, IMPACT, "Counterfeit Medicines: An Update On Estimates," November 15, 2006, www.who.int/medicines/services/counterfeit/impact/TheNew EstimatesCounterfeit.pdf; also, World Health Organization, "Counterfeit Medicines: fact sheet 275," November 14, 2006), www.who.int/mediacentre/factsheets/fs275/en/index.html; a. Associated Press, "Counterfeit Drugs Deemed Threat in Europe," September 22, 2005; and Joyce Primo-Carpenter and Milissa McGinnis, "Matrix of Drug Quality Reports in USAID-Assisted Countries" (U.S. Pharmacopeia, October 15, 2007), www.usp.org/pdf/EN/dqi/ghcDrugQuality Matrix.pdf; b. Coalition for Intellectual Property Rights (2003) as cited in Andrew Kramer, "Drug Piracy: A Wave of Counterfeit Medicines Washes Over Russia," *New York Times*, September 5, 2006.

NOTE: As the text discusses and the table illustrates, defining the prevalence of counterfeit drugs in the supply chain is difficult. Estimates are little more than educated guesses, and informed entities can and often do disagree.

In general, the market for fake drugs in developing countries tends to have a broader profile than in the industrialized world, with the types of drugs counterfeited being not only lifestyle drugs and painkillers but also lifesaving medicines, such as antiretrovirals for HIV/AIDS, antibiotics, and treatments for malaria and tuberculosis. Counterfeit antimalarial pills in the developing world are often quite sophisticated, and customers are easily duped into believing they are the real thing. There are often few distinguishing features between legitimate and fake pills, and sometimes the counterfeits are so well done that a consumer has almost no way to tell the difference.

As the near parity between the two packages in figure 1-2 illustrates, even the best-versed pharmaceutical security expert may have difficulty distinguishing between fake and real goods. For the average consumer—especially in impoverished nations, where information about medicine and disease is sparse—it is almost impossible. Most will not know what to look for to tell the two apart.

In 2002, Paul Newton of Oxford University reported in the *British Medical Journal* that 38 percent of antimalarial drugs bought in Southeast Asia, where malaria is still prevalent, were counterfeit.[32] (A more recent study discovered a much higher number: fully 68 percent of artesunate drugs collected in Laos, Burma, Vietnam, and Cambodia did not contain the correct amount of active ingredient.[33]) Some of the drugs Newton collected contained small amounts of acetaminophen, which temporarily lowers fevers but does not kill the malaria parasite. This effect convinces the patient that he is improving, when in fact a key symptom is merely being suppressed. As a result, the patient does not discover the drug is counterfeit until his illness is much worse.[34]

Drug counterfeiting in the developing world tends to be exacerbated by a lack of reliable statistics to accurately quantify the scope of the problem, inadequate regulatory structures, and consumer ignorance. Even so, unique political and economic conditions mean that the size and scope of the problem vary among regions and countries.

FIGURE 1-2

AUTHENTIC V. COUNTERFEIT VOVERAN (PAIN MEDICATION) PILLS

SOURCE: Author.
NOTE: The package on the left is authentic, while the package on the right is counterfeit.

Africa. The problem of counterfeit drugs is especially severe in sub-Saharan Africa. A 2005 study found that half the chloroquine tablets in some selected African countries contained incorrect levels of the active ingredient, rendering them ineffective; faulty chloroquine contributed to a doubling of malaria deaths in the areas under study.[35] While improvements have occurred in some places, such as Nigeria in the past few years (see "Stopping the Fakers," pages 46–48),[36] there is still a long way to go before the pharmaceutical markets in many African countries can be considered safe (see figure 1-3 on the following page).

One problem common to many developing countries is the persistent willingness, often driven by wretched poverty, of many

FIGURE 1-3

PERCENT FAILURE OF CHLOROQUINE (ANTIMALARIAL DRUG)
IN AFRICAN COUNTRIES

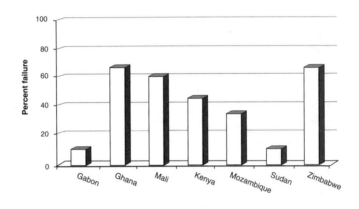

SOURCE: Charles Maponga and Clive Ondari, *The Quality of Antimalarials: A Study in Selected African Countries*, World Health Organization, 2003, http://whqlibdoc.who.int/hq/2003/WHO_EDM_PAR_2003.4.pdf (accessed March 17, 2008).

patients to buy drugs from street vendors or those selling drugs on doorsteps. In Burkina Faso, for example, where national regulations stipulate that consumers must buy medicines with a prescription, many consumers regularly buy drugs without them in street markets where counterfeits are common. According to the Ministry of Health, one in five pharmaceutical drugs bought in the capital city of Ouagadougou is counterfeit and sold without a prescription or expiration date.[37] Breaking the rules may be a rational decision for somebody who does not appreciate the risk, or cannot afford to travel to a proper pharmacy because the informal trader's goods will probably be cheaper and more readily available, often because they are not the real thing. Even branded products may be compromised by poor storage conditions—such as being held up on a quay by customs officials.[38] This may contribute to an inherent mistrust of

Western medicines and resentment of Western imports in some countries, and make a locally produced version more acceptable. This means that the poorest, least mobile, least educated people are the most vulnerable to fakes.

In Africa, where HIV/AIDS and malaria kill millions of people each year, the demand for medicine for these deadly diseases is enormous. Unfortunately, as a result of poverty, low literacy, and general ignorance, counterfeiters have been able to take advantage of desperation. In fact, many Africans will buy single pills at kiosks with no more packaging than handmade envelopes. Even in pharmacies, where blister packs (such as those in figure 1-2) are more likely to be available, there is close to no chance that a nonspecialist will have any knowledge about the correct appearance of the products. The customer must rely on the knowledge and integrity of the pharmacist.

In October 2007, a reporter for the news service Voice of America visited a street market in Dakar, Senegal. The market is effectively an unofficial pharmacy, and tables are piled high with boxes of medications. A vendor said that while he knew selling drugs in the market was illegal, he was not worried about getting caught. He believed he was providing a valuable service because many of his customers could not afford to go to the doctor to get prescriptions or buy from pharmacies. He added that police did not bother him because religious leaders protected his medicine sales.[39] The probability that these drugs were substandard or outright fakes was high. Even if the vendor's products were genuine, it is highly likely their efficacy would have been compromised by being exposed to the tropical West African climate day after day.

It is difficult to quantify the penetration of fake drugs in Africa because of the lack of data in many places. What is known is based on isolated studies, from which estimates are made as to the situation nationally. A 2002 study in Senegal found that twenty-one out of twenty-two samples of ampicillin (a common antibiotic) contained only flour.[40] Analysis of antimalarials in Angola, Burundi, and the Democratic Republic of Congo in 2006 discovered that 46 percent of drugs had been incorrectly formulated; and in more than 50 percent of cases, drugs were sold loose (without the original primary packaging, with the name of the active ingredient, strength, the expiry date, and, only in some cases, the producer's name and country written in pen), providing a ready opportunity for counterfeiting.[41] In Cameroon, a U.S. Pharmacopeia study found that 39 percent of samples had no active ingredients, insufficient active ingredients, or the wrong ingredients.[42] A survey in 2005 found that almost 30 percent of drugs in Kenya were counterfeit, with some being no more than chalk and water.[43] With counterfeit-drug sales estimated at $130 million every year, the costs of producing such fakes provide huge profit margins to the unscrupulous.[44]

Nigeria presented the worst case of drug counterfeiting in Africa until very recently when, under the leadership of its tough chief pharmaceutical regulator, Dora Akunyili, the country began taking significant action against counterfeiters (see pages 46–48). Consequently, the data from Nigeria are the most complete available, but even there, the beneficial impact of more rigorous oversight has not been consistently recorded.[45] Data vacuums persist. Still, customs investigations and simple studies of samples bought in markets, kiosks, and pharmacies in various countries are building a body of evidence about counterfeit drugs in Africa.

Latin America. The Pan American Health Organization (PAHO) has reported that home production, importation, and redistribution of counterfeits are increasing in Latin America. Illegal pharmaceuticals have been found in hospitals and pharmacies throughout Latin America, and increasingly, reports and discoveries are being made by pharmacists and doctors themselves. The reports are encouraging, but many patients continue to buy from street vendors or from the Pharmacia Similares, which sell not branded original medicines but copy medicines, which may include fake and substandard drugs.[46]

In addition, legitimate drugs are being stolen and their expiration dates extended so they can be reintroduced into the regular supply chain at a later date. The Dominican Republic's Ministry of Public Health reported in 2005 that about half of all pharmacies in that country were operating illegally, and 10 percent of medicines imported were fake. Some confiscated medicines had expired more than ten years earlier.[47] In March of the same year, investigators discovered an international network manufacturing fake tablets of Lipitor in Costa Rica for shipment to the United States, where they would have sold for some $8 million.

National pharmaceutical industry associations working with government organizations, PAHO, and each other report similar experiences. Sales of counterfeit, contraband, or adulterated drugs in Colombia in 2004 were estimated to be worth $60 million, representing 5 percent of all drugs sold in the country. The Association of Pharmaceutical Laboratories of Peru reported a market worth $66 million in 2006—up from $40 million in 2002. Manufacturers in El Salvador estimate the losses to legitimate laboratories to have been $40 million in 2005. Illegal pharmaceutical products represent about 10 percent of Mexico's market.[48]

Russia. One of the world's largest "gray" economies is Russia's, and pharmaceutical businesses are fully integrated into it. The *Lancet* reports that drug manufacturers often run legally by day but add extra shifts at night "to produce extra quantities of a certified drug that does not pass through quality control, or sophisticated copies of well-known drugs are produced, often with reduced levels of expensive active ingredients. These fakes can be exact copies or put in packaging where only a letter or two is altered on the name."[49]

Counterfeits produced on the side are then channeled to Russia's domestic market and, occasionally, to Europe and the United States. Counterfeit-drug production is worth an estimated $300 million per year in Russia, and although the government claims counterfeiting is decreasing,[50] it admits that up to 10 percent of medicines are still faked. The Coalition for Intellectual Property Rights gives a higher estimate of 12 percent.[51]

Russia's underground market is characterized by unusually well-made fakes, according to private investigators from Pfizer who surveyed the Russian market in 2006.[52] A decade ago, many fakes in Russia were produced in basements and backrooms, but most now come from the night shift at legitimate pharmaceutical companies.

About 70 percent of fake drugs in circulation in Russia are produced inside the country, and an estimated 70 percent of these are copies of foreign medications.[53] Although thus far it appears that quality has remained high, there is no incentive for counterfeiters to maintain quality, especially since counterfeiting is only a civil liability, not a criminal one, and the fines are negligible.[54]

Political corruption and bureaucratic complacency in Russia have allowed the counterfeit-drug trade to flourish. "We have had people in the regional governments even saying about improper medicines, 'What's wrong with that, the quality is super and we're going to buy it,'" says Gennady Shirshov, executive director of Russia's Union of Professional Pharmaceutical Organizations (SPFO).[55] But, recently, there has been a shift. Russian authorities are just now realizing the extent of the danger illegal drugs can pose to health. While they have no statistics on the harm caused to patients by fake drugs, and it is still generally thought that the sufficient—if not good—quality of most of them has prevented deaths, they are becoming alarmed by the possibility that about 45 percent of counterfeits in Russia are medicines for serious cardiovascular or gastrointestinal illnesses.

The problem in Russia is especially hard to deal with because those engaging in faking are protected, and some are extremely influential and powerful. Vladimir Bryntsalov, a member of parliament and billionaire pharmaceutical magnate who once ran for president, is currently under investigation, charged with collecting 54 million rubles ($2.1 million) from illicit sales of medicinal alcohol. Bryntsalov's company, Bryntsalov-A, and its subsidiary Ferein, however, also produce up to 10 percent of Russia's legitimate pharmaceuticals. Producers like Bryntsalov (and others allegedly linked to the Russian mafia) operate both in and out of the shadows, using their legal status to obtain raw materials that can then be diverted through channels not subject to stringent regulation.[56] There have so far been no successful prosecutions of any senior figure involved in counterfeiting.

In addition to being produced in-country, counterfeit and substandard drugs are being imported into Russia at increasing rates. According to sources in India,[57] exports from India to countries in the Commonwealth of Independent States, including Russia, are increasing, with cross-border associations of narcotic and fake drug traffickers between Russia and India flourishing.

Asia. India is the source of most substandard active pharmaceutical ingredients and counterfeit drugs in the world, with China not far behind. Joined by Pakistan and the Mekong River Valley countries, and enabled by the region's myriad, unregulated small producers (by some estimates, India has 22,000 drug producers, most with annual revenues under $100 million), Asia might be considered the fake factory of the world. According to the European Commission's 2006 report, 31 percent of fake medicines imported into the EU came from India, 31 percent from the United Arab Emirates, and 20 percent from China.[58] This is alarming for western nations such as the United States, given that an estimated 20 percent of generic drugs in the United States come from India or China, and more than 40 percent of the active ingredients of drugs made in the United States come from one of these two countries. Analysts estimate that, within fifteen years, this figure may increase to more than 80 percent.[59]

Thus far, relatively rigorous import controls in the United States, coupled with what appears to be self-regulation on the exporting side (an assumption based on the low incidence of fakes despite the high volume of imports), appear to have prevented any significant influx of faulty products;[60] all the same, the opportunity for compromise in the system is worrisome, especially as organized crime and terrorist organizations increasingly become involved.

While data on markets affected by exports from these countries are plentiful, if unsystematic, information on the penetration of counterfeit and substandard drugs within them is difficult to find. Some of the best documentation available is on the website of WHO's International Medical Products Anti-Counterfeiting Taskforce (IMPACT).[61] In India's major cities, IMPACT reports, one in five medicines sold in the period under investigation was a fake. India's pharmaceutical companies claimed a loss in revenue of between 4 and 5 percent annually. The industry also estimated that illegal drugs had grown from 10 percent to 20 percent of the total market. Other observers, including investigators hired by domestic and multinational pharmaceutical companies, say fakes range from 5 percent in some markets to as much as 30 percent in others.[62] Yet the official estimate of the Indian government, as reported by WHO, of "spurious" drugs (as fakes are known in India), is less than 1 percent, with substandard drugs comprising less than 10 percent.[63] China's research and development–based pharmaceutical association has estimated that about 8 percent of over-the-counter drugs sold in China are counterfeit.[64]

Not surprisingly, many poorer countries in Southeast Asia, with geographical proximity to the myriad counterfeit producers of China and India, and without the economic and political leverage or enforcement power of wealthier markets (like Japan), are awash in counterfeit drugs. As aforementioned, a 2006 study found that 68 percent of artesunate drugs collected in Laos, Burma, Vietnam, and Cambodia did not contain the correct amount of active ingredient.[65]

Although fake drug markets in developing countries are varied, they undoubtedly flourish in numerous locations and share similar attributes. Any drug type can and will be faked based on market potential for the fakers, which varies from market to market and according to the presence of effective deterrents. Where politicians have shown no political will to tackle the problem, the problem is increasing. But it is not insurmountable, and where authorities have demonstrated a willingness to enforce controls more rigorously and crack down on counterfeiters, the problem is diminishing.

2

How and Why Does
Counterfeiting Occur?

Counterfeiting happens because it is both highly lucrative—particularly for goods with low marginal costs of production, such as pharmaceutical drugs or electronics—and convenient. Little consumer awareness coupled with weak regulatory structures means that most counterfeiters are never discovered. Insufficiently punitive penalties mean that consequences tend to be minimal for those who are caught. Together, these elements make counterfeiting pharmaceuticals a relatively high-reward, low-risk enterprise.

Incentives to Counterfeit

Like other counterfeit products, counterfeit pharmaceuticals exist because there is a big market for the authentic original product and because profit margins on sales of the counterfeits are high. Medicinal counterfeiters exploit the often high prices of genuine drugs.

Real pharmaceuticals can be expensive for many reasons. The popular, if ill-informed, view is that greedy multinationals want to squeeze the last penny out of the sick and dying. Of course, there are many bona fide reasons for prices to be far higher than marginal cost. Research and development costs are the most obvious. Although patents are designed to allow these costs to be recovered, they have to be filed very early on in the process, so by the time a drug reaches the market (if it does at all), the period of protection may be too short to recoup the company's investment. Technical factors also push up costs. Active ingredients may be expensive or difficult to acquire. The sweet wormwood plant (*Artemisia annua*), which is the basis of the newest antimalarial drugs, is a case in point. The plant takes fourteen months to grow—a very long time in a market whose value is uncertain because antimalarials are often donated or sold below cost. Companies take on futures contracts with farmers, often in unstable countries, and they are subject to foreign exchange risks as well as the whims of the international donors that support the market.

But these issues are of little interest to copiers and counterfeiters— and activists, for that matter—who consider only the retail price of the drug. Counterfeiters who do not care if they use any active ingredient at all and manufacturers who are not fussy about the niceties of WHO's good manufacturing practice (GMP) guidelines can exploit the margin and rake in easy profits—provided their products look good enough to pass for the real thing, and their tracks are covered.[1]

Further incentive to counterfeit is provided by tensions between pharmaceutical companies and the governments of developing countries. While developing countries do take some action to deter out-and-out counterfeits, conflict between public health and industrial drive may lead governments to protect nascent drug industries by promoting domestic companies that produce copy drugs (especially for export), even though the quality of such products may be poor. India, for example, has more stringent regulations for drugs consumed domestically than those that are exported. Substandard drugs from government-backed entities in developing countries constitute a major problem that may discourage the involvement of higher-quality foreign suppliers.[2] And as the number of legitimate suppliers that produce poor-quality drugs increases, it becomes easier for those trading fakes to introduce their wares into the market. When combined with Internet pharmacies, porous borders, colluding wholesalers, poor consumer awareness, and—crucially— weak detection systems and ridiculously low penalties, these conditions make counterfeiting alluring to criminals, as well as to legitimate manufacturing laboratories that operate on the fringes of legality. With lax regulation and control of GMP, manufacturers may cut corners and produce substandard medicines—making extra production runs a side business that may involve adulterating, diluting, repackaging, and relabeling drugs to misrepresent dosage, origin, or expiration date.[3]

Corruption within Countries

Outright corruption in various forms and at different levels within countries worsens and possibly facilitates the counterfeit problem. According to Maureen Lewis, a senior economist at the World Bank, corruption in the health sector is rife.[4] This is true in rich as well as poorer countries, but better reporting systems, the threat of litigation, and higher incomes for health professionals vastly reduce the problem in the wealthier ones. In the developing world, on the other hand, corrupt practices in the health-care sector often force patients to pay directly for drugs that are supposed to be free at point of use. This encourages patients to choose the cheapest drugs available, which are more likely to be fake or substandard. In the middle-income and poor countries of Moldova, Sri Lanka, Morocco, and many others, more than 80 percent of the public thinks the health-care sector is corrupt, with "informal" payments for drugs common.[5]

A plethora of private, unlicensed sellers also enables the counterfeit drug problem. In Ethiopia, for example, there is rampant stealing of public-sector drugs, which are then resold in the private market. In 2003, researchers in Nigeria found a significant rate of non-payment to medical staff, and concluded that "the greater the average number of months of salary non-payment in a facility . . . the greater the probability that essential drugs (chloroquine, paracetamol, and antibiotics) [were] privately provided by facility staff rather than being facility owned."[6] According to a 2001 study cited by a Center for Global Development report, over 50 percent of drugs had gone missing from public medical facilities in two states in Nigeria.[7] According to a 1999 estimate from Uganda, over 70 percent of drugs in the public sector went missing during the period of one year.[8] While these drugs may be produced according to GMP, their diversion through the hands of unlicensed drug sellers—who may be uninformed or inept at distribution—may render them ineffective.

Many health workers are involved in corruption within the health care systems, partly due to their low pay. Rafael Di Tella and William D. Savedoff studied seven Latin American countries and found routine overpayment for supplies—including drugs—due to gross mismanagement and corruption. Given the enormous margins fakes can provide to those involved in their trade, corruption in the drug supply chain nearly always involves fakes or substandard drugs. Other problems, from petty theft of drugs by nurses and doctors to widespread "leakage," reveal myriad vast holes through which fake and substandard drugs enter middle-income and poor countries.[9] Solutions to such problems may be rooted in reducing corruption in the public sector rather than attempting to combat fake drugs directly.[10]

Complex Supply Chains Encourage Fakes

It stands to reason that any complex system with many interchangeable parts is especially susceptible to being breached—it has more vulnerabilities than a simpler system. This applies to the pharmaceutical supply chain. Having a secure source of sound drugs is no guarantee of safety if the supply chain is full of weaknesses and holes. Today's supply chains offer many openings to counterfeiters, from diffuse and little-regulated wholesale systems in the United States and the EU to misguided trade barriers in developing countries.

Developed Countries. In developed economies, the supply chain between producer and consumer is short and, for the most part, secure. In the United States, 98 percent of the nation's medicine is distributed through wholesalers. Of these medicines, 90 percent are distributed by the "Big Three"—Cardinal, AmeriSourceBergen, and McKesson—all longstanding, trusted channels. But another layer of wholesalers—about 6,500—forms a secondary market that buys and sells surplus medicine and is responsible for approximately

$9.3 billion worth of drugs.[11] These further subdivisions improve efficiency, industry insiders say. Regional wholesalers, for instance, have contacts with distributors in certain regions of the country, and even smaller wholesalers specialize in storing and delivering one or two kinds of drugs.

But this is the stage in the supply chain at which counterfeiters can most readily insert themselves, claiming they are wholesalers who receive drugs from other wholesalers. A drug is passed from the manufacturer to a wholesaler, which can then distribute it to even more wholesalers—maybe as many as five between manufacturer and pharmacist[12]—channeling it into a loosely regulated market in which legitimate wholesalers may trade willingly or unwittingly with counterfeiters posing as wholesalers. Drugmakers, Congress, and law enforcement agencies have long complained that counterfeiters posing as small wholesalers practice "diversion," substituting fake medicines with phony paperwork and realistic packaging into shipments en route to pharmacies and hospitals. In these cases, the authentic drugs diverted from the shipments are then resold. In other cases, even legitimate wholesalers may buy drugs from counterfeiters, believing they are getting a better bargain.[13]

Margins are so tight in the distribution chain, however, that prices more than 10 percent lower than expected anywhere along the supply chain should be treated with suspicion by middlemen, retailers, and pharmacists buying the products.[14] At times the pharmacy, by buying the drugs at or below cost in hopes of making a greater profit, is willfully (or at least tacitly) complicit in the counterfeiting scheme.[15]

It is remarkably easy for someone to become a licensed wholesaler; sometimes fees are less than $1,000. Once licensed, wholesalers can legally buy and sell pharmaceuticals in the supply chain. In Miami, for example, the owner of an auto body shop received a license to be a drug wholesaler in Maryland.[16] And in Nevada, a twenty-three-year-old restaurant hostess received a license to operate an online pharmacy.[17]

Many of these small wholesalers operate out of homes and garages and are subject to little federal regulatory oversight;

state-level oversight is spotty and inconsistent, too. In Florida, for example, one needs only a refrigerator, an air conditioner, an alarm to secure products, a $200 security bond, and a $700 license to become a wholesale distributor.[18] Tracking these small distributors is a huge task that local law enforcement officials, usually under pressure to investigate higher-profile narcotics crimes, have been unable to confront.[19] Maryland has seven inspectors for 632 wholesalers, and Virginia has nine inspectors for 684 wholesalers.[20] In Florida, a nexus for the illicit pharmaceutical trade in the United States, nine drug inspectors regulate 2,699 businesses.[21] With such low staffing levels, the regulation of even registered companies slips—much less the interdiction of unregistered operations. One FDA official estimated that companies that should be checked every one to two years were instead checked every eight to ten.[22]

The FDA's inspection of foreign drug producers is even less comprehensive, inhibited by a lack of resources, international legal norms, and the agency's own poor recordkeeping mechanisms. A Government Accountability Office report released in October 2007 found that the FDA inspected 7 percent of all foreign manufacturing establishments approved to export medicines to the United States in a given year—meaning that it would take the agency more than thirteen years to inspect each establishment just once. Inspections themselves were problematic. Most tended to be tied to a given facility's application to market a new drug, rather than focused on facilities manufacturing drugs already on the market; they were not unannounced and could not easily be extended if problems were encountered; and the FDA did not provide translators, forcing some inspection teams to rely on English-speaking representatives of the foreign establishments. Finally, the FDA lacks a systematic database tracking all foreign establishments. One database indicates there are about 3,000 foreign establishments registered to produce drugs marketed in the United States; another indicates about 6,800.[23]

Consumer vigilance remains low because many Americans do not even know the drug wholesale system exists. According to a 2006 Opinion Research Corporation poll commissioned by the National Consumers League, 37 percent of Americans incorrectly

Figure 2-1
Drug Supply Chains

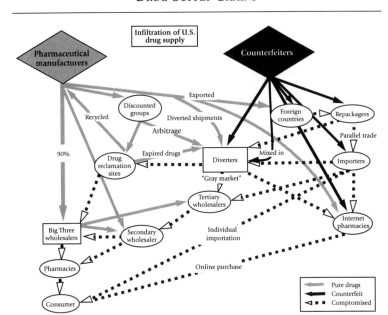

SOURCE: Wyatt Yankus, *Counterfeit Drugs: Coming to a Pharmacy Near You*, American Council on Science and Health, 2006, available at www.acsh.org/publications/pubID.1379/pub_detail.asp (accessed March 20, 2008).

NOTE: This diagram depicts the complexity of the drug supply chain and the number of times a single drug can change hands as it travels from the manufacturer to the customer. The dotted lines represent the different routes by which counterfeit drugs can enter the U.S. supply chain and make their way to American consumers.

think that prescription drugs go directly from manufacturers to the pharmacy shelves.[24]

There is even more complexity in the European Union, which operates a system called parallel trading under which it is legal to buy drugs cheaply in one part of Europe and sell them at a higher price in another part. In economics, this process of taking advantage of price differences for a profit is known as arbitrage. Arbitrage generally increases efficiency because it corrects for price discrepancies within and across markets. In practical terms, this is true for pharmaceuticals, too. But arbitrage lowers efficiency in the drug market because the market is unusual; its products require extensive R&D but are cheap to produce, so an efficient level of pricing is above marginal cost in wealthier markets.[25] By increasing the number of hands that drugs pass through in the supply chain, arbitrage raises the chances that counterfeits are able to infiltrate it.

Another weakness in the chain is the network of wholesalers who specialize in fulfilling cross-border transactions. For example, drugs need to carry consumer instructions in the language of the country in which they are to be sold, on paper and on the drug blister packets, as well as on outer packaging. This (legitimately) requires instructions to be translated and reprinted and calls for new packaging to be prepared by middlemen. As discussed in chapter 1, packaging is one of the primary means by which counterfeiters can insert themselves into supply chains. The European repackaging process gives them just this opportunity. A counterfeiter posing as a parallel-trade intermediary, for instance, could claim that he legitimately purchased a drug in a Spanish-speaking country, repackaged it into English, and then sold it in the United Kingdom—when in reality he bought the drug in another country with less stringent manufacturing requirements than the Spanish-speaking country, such as India. This scenario played itself out in May 2007, when the United Kingdom's Medical and Healthcare Products Regulatory Agency was forced to recall batches of fake schizophrenia and hypertension drugs after they were discovered to have been counterfeited with forged French packaging.[26] Similarly, in July 2005, the MHRA found 70 packets of counterfeit Lipitor in the facilities of two different UK wholesalers. The packets had proper identification numbers, but this was only because the packaging had been forged. Around 2,500 packets of fake Lipitor had already been distributed in the National Health Service supply chain before MHRA's discovery.[27]

Important differences exist among the counterfeit-drug markets in different countries in Europe. According to UK officials, for example, the British drug supply chain is one of the safest in the world, with counterfeits accounting for only about 1 percent of the market.[28] Still, they, like other European countries, have found themselves increasingly susceptible to the infiltration of fakes. French customs agents, for instance, reported seizing 542,000 fake drugs in 2005.[29] Finland appears to have a large counterfeit problem. In early 2007, Finnish customs officials confiscated 140,000 counterfeit drugs entering the country,[30] a sizable number for a population of 5.2 million.[31] An obvious contributing factor is Finland's long Russian border,[32] along with its lax transit laws, which currently allow for the unrestricted transit of medicines, with shipments of imported medicine investigated only if the patent-holder of a particular medicine files a complaint with Finnish officials.

Developing Countries. For anyone who has tried to clear an item through customs in developing countries, the endless paperwork and bureaucratic heavy-handedness are all too familiar. A *Customs Modernization Handbook* published by the World Bank lists eleven separate steps necessary to clear customs in most countries.[33] Throw into this burdensome mix poorly paid and occasionally unscrupulous customs agents, as well as irregular tariff systems in which no one seems to know the exact rates or bothers to look them up, and corruption is almost inevitable.

The link between tariffs and corruption is clear.[34] Tariffs provide opportunities for irregular payments, and they delay product shipment. Frequently altered tariff rates create opportunities for public officials to extract bribes. Local officials often have exclusive knowledge about the "correct" fees and possess the authority to change them locally, giving them improper leverage. In some cases, they waive official fees in exchange for bribes.

Capricious intervention by customs officials leaves importers with little choice but to pay bribes to avoid delays, especially when goods with short shelf-lives (for example, antibiotics and other drugs that need refrigeration) are concerned. Such corruption contributes to the instability of access to medicines in these countries.

Tariffs and the corruption associated with them also cause problems for humanitarian organizations. The U.S.-based Catholic Medical Mission Board (CMMB), a leading provider of global health care, donates approximately $175 million in pharmaceuticals each year to over fifty countries in approximately five hundred different shipments. CMMB crosses many borders and is familiar with customs operations around the world. One would think such humanitarian shipments would be exempt from duties and customs clearance fees. But each time CMMB brings goods into a country, it is asked by customs officials to pay questionable "administrative handling fees" for documentation filings in proportion to the statistical value of the shipment. In Vietnam, for example, some form of payment is regularly demanded of CMMB upon the entry of its donated medicines.

CMMB is not alone in its experience. Private companies are often required to pay significant taxes and tariffs, even for drugs they price at marginal cost, and in some instances for drugs donated for free (in these cases, a price is imputed based on some reference price). Janssen-Cilag, a research and pharmaceutical company based in the United Kingdom, reports that it frequently pays import duties and value-added taxes, plus a premium, on drugs it sells in Burma, leading to a price markup of an additional 15–20 percent.[35]

Gilead Sciences, a biopharmaceutical company, had its global-outreach commitment tested in 2004 and 2005 when drugs shipped to Kenya, Uganda, and South Africa were held up in ports. In one case, a drug shipment meant for Médecins Sans Frontières (MSF, known in English as Doctors without Borders) treatment programs in South Africa was repeatedly delayed. To make matters worse, MSF—which is primarily in the business of providing medical care—was ill-equipped to tackle the bureaucratic requirements of obtaining permits and securing prepayments for the release of the drugs, leading to even greater delays. After three years the situation was resolved, but only after the services of local distributors had been secured. Some Gilead officials remarked that such hurdles are a significant deterrent to their ongoing commitment to the region.[36]

Not all drug supply efforts have met with this frustrating opposition. Larger donors, such as the President's Emergency Plan for AIDS Relief and the U.S. Agency for International Development, have successfully demanded that tariffs and all forms of nonofficial payments be suspended for their donations. Other agencies and groups, however, have not had the same luck. Unlike aid from EU member countries, a significant amount of American foreign aid is disbursed by private organizations, which means it is not exempt from tariffs.[37]

Sometimes developed-world hostility can threaten productive trade relationships. China's charge of Western media manipulation of its counterfeit problem, though largely a defensive measure, appears to have some truth to it—many Western media outlets and politicians probably have reacted unfairly to reports of dangerous Chinese goods.[38] Rhetoric that raises suspicion without sound evidence not only distorts the size of the problem; it threatens the beneficial trade relationship between the developing and developed worlds. It is important to remember that the threat posed by counterfeits can only be countered by mutual cooperation. An overreaction to the reports of the flow of dangerous goods coming out of developing countries may undermine future efforts to reduce it.

Counterfeiting, Organized Crime, and Terrorism

Because the counterfeit-drug industry is a highly profitable enterprise, especially in environments of weak regulation and enforcement where penalties are slight, it has attracted organized criminal groups like the Russian mafia, Chinese triads, Colombian cocaine traffickers, and the Mexican mafia.[39] Francis Burnett of the Caribbean Industrial Research Institute points out that many of these groups were driven from narcotrafficking to the counterfeit-drug trade because of the potential for high profits, with comparatively low risk.[40] This movement was accelerated by antidrug efforts that increased the potential costs relative to benefits from trafficking in narcotics. "Petty criminals, but especially organized criminals, have identified [counterfeiting licit drugs] as a way to make big bucks and with lower penalties than cocaine or crack or heroin," says Lewis Kontnick of Reconnaissance International, a Denver-based consulting firm that works on counterfeiting issues.[41] As Jim Christian, head of corporate security for the drugmaker Novartis, comments, "If you get caught with a pound of cocaine, you can expect to do serious time. But if you are found with counterfeit medicines, you might do only six months."[42] In May 2001, for example, drug officials in Colombia discovered a counterfeit manufacturing ring in a poor neighborhood of Bogotá. Workers were producing more than 20,000 counterfeit versions a day of the flu drug Dristan. The ten people caught in the act and arrested were free on bail within a few days.[43]

Stiffer penalties alone will not solve the counterfeiting problem. As Randy Barnett, a law professor at Boston University and a former criminal prosecutor for the Cook County State's Attorney's Office in Chicago, explains, the deterrent power of potential punishment is a function of both its severity *and* the rate of prosecution (that is, the likelihood of getting caught and convicted). A government's first response to counterfeiting often involves increasing fines, periods of incarceration, and other forms of punishment.[44] Although a strong step, the stiffer punishment may not have the desired effect. By increasing penalties, a government may unwittingly decrease the likely rate of prosecution, thereby canceling or even reversing any added deterrence. In the United States, for example, convictions in criminal trials demand evidence "beyond reasonable doubt"; verdicts in civil trials permit a less rigorous "preponderance of the evidence." In criminal trials for serious offenses, where punishments may be severe, the evidence hypothetically is held to the highest standard. Even when a criminal is successfully prosecuted, punishment in high-stakes cases may be delayed, further weakening the penalty's deterrent power.[45]

Harsher penalties also increase incentives for counterfeiters to resist capture and prosecution. Potential defendants may bribe or intimidate officials, especially customs agents. If a trial seems likely, they will pay for better lawyers and may invest in buying off witnesses. While some potential counterfeiters may be deterred, those who remain will tend to be more organized and more violent. Making punishment more severe is usually a step in the right direction, but only when it is joined with strong enforcement.[46]

And the counterfeit problem extends far beyond the merely criminal. In 2004, the departing U.S. secretary of health and human services, Tommy Thompson, highlighted the vulnerability of Western markets to counterfeits used by terrorist organizations, not so much to cause direct injury and panic as to fund straightforward terrorist actions.[47] In March 2006, the U.S. Joint Terrorism Task Force—an interagency initiative led by the FBI—charged nineteen people with operating a counterfeit-drug ring that spanned Lebanon, Canada, China, Brazil, Paraguay, and the United States. Profits from the sales of counterfeits and other contraband were used to support the terrorist group Hezbollah.[48] Previously, counterfeiting had been viewed by most authorities solely as an intellectual property issue—something that might damage profits and brand credibility but had little effect on anyone other than the patent-holder. But Ronald Noble, the current secretary general of Interpol, the world's largest international police organization, warns that "intellectual property crime"—which includes counterfeiting medicines—"is becoming the preferred method of funding for a number of terrorist groups."[49] At a meeting with WHO's department of essential medicines and policy in 2005, Interpol intelligence officer Erik Madsen noted that emerging evidence showed links between counterfeiting and organized crime and terrorist organizations, including al Qaeda.[50] Fighting fake drugs requires calm, reasoned action, but the response must take on the urgency warranted by these developments.

Conclusion

While it is clear from the aforementioned examples that counterfeit and substandard drugs affect people across the globe and have entered supply chains in many developed countries, much uncertainty remains about the precise extent and character of the problem. Although the appearance of fakes in the United States and Britain is disconcerting, few cases of deadly counterfeits have been reported in either country. July 2007 marked the first time a death in the developed world was officially linked to counterfeit pharmaceuticals purchased over the Internet.[51] Canadian investigators found e-mail records showing that over several months in 2006, fifty-eight-year-old Marcia Bergeron had unwittingly purchased counterfeit antidepressants and acetaminophen from several unlicensed online pharmacies. The drugs, which contained dangerously high levels of aluminum, phosphorus, titanium, tin, strontium, arsenic, and other metals, ultimately killed her.

The threads of modern drug counterfeiting stretch around the world and from the top to the bottom of the international community—from rural Chinese workshops to large retail pharmacies; from Interpol to street hawkers. Those involved in or affected by counterfeiting are disaggregated groups with disparate interests. Even where there is a will to take action, coordination is difficult. The middle-aged American man buying fake Viagra from a fraudulent online pharmacy has the FDA to look after his interests; the poor African mother unknowingly buying fake malaria medicine in single doses for her baby is more deserving of protection, but receives none.

Some local authorities, especially in the developing world, tolerate domestic fakers, viewing them as Robin Hoods robbing rich foreign firms to heal the poor. Some international aid agencies tolerate substandard drugs that are produced by small, local firms as a way to "improve competition."[52] But these perspectives should be tolerated only as long as these drugs do not pose a threat to patients' health.

Counterfeiters do not usually have long-term business plans; they exploit opportunities for profit for as long as they provide better returns than the next best alternative. Many world markets are effectively unguarded, and the chances of detection or punishment are negligible. The lack of credible deterrents draws the professional criminal from more dangerous activities. Even legitimate actors involved in manufacturing and distribution may be tempted to moonlight. Regulation has yet to seriously mitigate the activities of counterfeiters; enforcement of existing regulation remains lax. If and when regulations are enforced, criminals may respond violently, with the same level of aggression found in the war on narcotics.

3

Stopping the Fakers

Although eradication of counterfeits is neither efficient nor possible, steps are being taken to decrease its prevalence, particularly in the area of medicine. Some are being implemented at the national level, others by international organizations. Equally important are steps being taken by private parties, such as pharmaceutical companies and pharmacists.

At the International Level

Among multilateral actors, the World Health Organization has spearheaded the movement to crack down on drug counterfeiting. The agency's International Conference on Combating Counterfeit Medicines, held in February 2006 in Rome, led to the Declaration of Rome, in which the global community recognized drug counterfeiting as a "vile and serious criminal offence that puts human lives at risk and undermines the credibility of health systems."[1]

At the conference, members pledged to work together to address the global challenge of drug counterfeiting through the creation of the International Medical Products Anti-Counterfeiting Taskforce. IMPACT includes representatives from all the major anticounterfeiting players, including intergovernmental organizations, nongovernmental organizations, enforcement agencies, pharmaceutical manufacturers' associations, and national drug and regulatory authorities.[2] The role of enforcement within IMPACT is undertaken by Interpol, the world's largest international police organization. As part of its partnership with IMPACT, Interpol has so far built partnerships with countries in Latin America, Southeast Asia, and Africa to train police in combating counterfeit drug–smuggling networks, coordinating police operations, and tracking the flow of fake drugs.[3]

IMPACT aims to build coordinated networks across and among countries to halt the production, trading, and selling of fake medicines around the globe by

- raising awareness among international organizations and other stakeholders to improve cooperation in combating counterfeit medicines;

- raising awareness among national authorities and decision-makers and calling for effective legislative measures to combat counterfeit medicines;

- establishing effective information exchanges and providing assistance on specific issues related to combating counterfeit medicines;

- developing technical and administrative tools to support the establishment or strengthening of international, regional, and national strategies; and

- encouraging coordination among anticounterfeiting initiatives.[4]

IMPACT has made some progress toward these goals. It has increased awareness of the dangers of counterfeit medical products and has been a forum for anticounterfeiting initiatives. It spearheaded a task force in Lisbon in December 2007 on developing effective anticounterfeiting legislation and helped orchestrate a February 2008 meeting among technology developers, drug manufacturers, and regulators to discuss using technology to combat counterfeit drugs. Still, because IMPACT must function through existing national structures and institutions—many of which have proved incapable of combating fakes—its influence may be limited, especially given WHO's poor record of standing up to individual nations with poor policies. In 2004, for example, before IMPACT was formed, WHO withdrew eighteen antiretrovirals from its pre-qualification list, and no member state required any of the companies involved to do a product recall (although one company, Ranbaxy, voluntarily did so).

At the National Level

IMPACT aims to build networks that work through national governments which, theoretically, have the legal authority and regulatory power to act on anticounterfeiting initiatives. In practice, however, both the practical ability and political will for combating counterfeiting vary widely from country to country. Some countries have stringent national drug regulatory authorities—such as the U.S. Food and Drug Administration or the EU's European Medicines Agency (EMEA)—while others have poorly functioning or less efficient regulatory authorities, or none at all. Legal frameworks in different countries define counterfeiting in different ways, or fail to address it at all. Argentina, for example, has no law against counterfeiting. Some aspects of counterfeiting may be specific to particular countries or regions. While national governments can benefit from the knowledge-sharing and coordination of international partnerships like IMPACT, each must confront counterfeiting as it happens on its own home turf.

Developed Countries. Pharmaceutical counterfeiting of the international scope and sophistication observed today—often featuring high-quality fakes produced in poorer, relatively unregulated countries and targeted at developed countries' lucrative markets—is relatively new, and governments in developed countries are still coming to grips with how best to confront it. Japan, the United States, and the European Union have focused on monitoring imports and improving customs control.

Japan. With the third-largest pharmaceutical market after North America and Europe,[5] Japan represents a lucrative opportunity for counterfeiters. Since 2002, the country has worked to streamline and strengthen its regulatory system, by amending its Pharmaceutical Affairs Law (PAL) to include a risk-based classification for products, revised manufacturing controls and quality assurance standards, and increased postmarketing surveillance. In April 2005, the government established a separate entity, the Pharmaceuticals and Medical Devices Agency (PMDA), to promote a more efficient and transparent drug review and approval process.[6] Under PAL, PMDA is required to conduct GMP inspections globally. It has announced plans to hire 150 inspectors and has sought assistance from the pharmaceutical industry to train them. Prior to 2004, all individuals importing medicines "for business purposes" were required to be licensed by the government;[7] under PAL, the government has strengthened these requirements, calling for any business to be physically located in Japan and have three controllers, one each for safety, quality assurance, and general purposes. To gain approval to market new drugs, companies must demonstrate an ability to guarantee the safety, quality, and efficacy of the product, as well as compliance with good quality, manufacturing, and vigilance practices for manufacturing sites and for products already on the market.[8] These initiatives combine strong regulatory requirements with important company-level responsibility.

Nevertheless, as noted by Paul D'Eramo, chairman of the International Society of Pharmaceutical Engineering's regulatory affairs committee, "It is difficult to know how the new law will be interpreted and enforced by the government."[9] As of February 2007, for example, Japan had hired only 28 of the 150 planned inspectors. Other critics say the official Japanese requirements may be too rigorous, discouraging efficient international trade with unnecessary rules and regulations. In a report released in March 2007, the U.S. International Trade Commission noted that between 2001 and 2005, the average time required to approve new medical devices was higher in Japan than in other principal global markets, including the United States and the European Union. Although the 2005 PAL reforms made some strides in reducing these times, "significant challenges" remain.[10]

FIGURE 3-1

COUNTERFEIT DRUG CASES OPENED BY THE FDA, 1997–2006

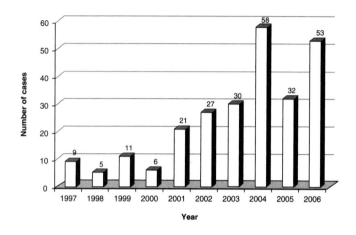

SOURCE: U.S. Food and Drug Administration, "Counterfeit Drug Cases Opened by Fiscal Year," http://www.fda.gov/oc/initiatives/counterfeit/hdmanadcs1113_files/textmostly/slide3.html (accessed August 3, 2007).

United States. The U.S. Food and Drug Administration is the chief pharmaceutical monitoring agency in the United States, responsible not only for the approval of drugs for mass distribution, but also for informing citizens of the threat posed by counterfeit drugs and providing regulatory oversight for drug production. In recent years, the FDA has stepped up enforcement of counterfeit-drug operations inside and outside of the country. In 2004, the FDA's Office of Criminal Investigations (OCI) opened fifty-eight counterfeit-drug criminal cases, up from thirty in 2003 (see figure 3-1 above). Most of the drugs confiscated by the FDA in these cases were headed to the black market or online pharmacies.[11]

In 2004, U.S. customs officials collected 3,000 packages suspected of containing counterfeit or unapproved drugs. An analysis of 180 of the packages revealed that 67 percent contained drugs that either were never approved by the FDA or had been withdrawn from the U.S. market for safety reasons. The drugs in 5 percent of the packages had no active ingredient, and 28 percent contained controlled substances banned from importation into the United States.[12]

The FDA has constructed a system in which it can focus attention on the riskiest imports. "Intelligent, risk-based inspections are more important than absolute numbers of inspections," the FDA announced in a June 2007 statement.[13] The OCI has been responsible for the convictions of several Americans engaged in illegal pharmaceutical smuggling and production over the past five years, including some people involved with Chinese counterfeiters.[14]

The FDA also issues and monitors the National Drug Code (NDC) Directory, an index of bar codes required on all pharmaceutical packaging. The NDC identifies the drug and includes such information as dosage form, active ingredients, and strength, allowing pharmacists and patients to differentiate among look-alike drugs in order to prevent prescription error. The FDA requires pharmaceutical firms to update their NDC information in June or December of each year. Drugs ordered over the Internet or sold in certain pharmacies, however, may not have an NDC barcode or be registered in the system, and many consumers may not know to ask for this information.

Increasingly, the FDA is also working to place inspectors at the point of production. In March 2008, Secretary of Health and Human Services Mike Leavitt announced that the FDA had begun negotiations with the Indian government to station officials in the country in order to check the safety of products bound for the United States. This was a "high priority," Leavitt said, given that more FDA approvals had been coming out of that country than any other in the world.[15] Congress has scheduled several hearings to consider further expanding the FDA's investigative presence abroad.[16]

European Union. Europe's parallel-trading system,[17] designed to make Europe a de facto single market for pharmaceuticals, relies on national systems to maintain the security of pharmaceutical trading. To protect against the growing volume of counterfeits on the

Internet and in European supply chains, drugs in the parallel-trading system can be bought and sold only in licensed pharmacies. Some European countries have attempted to regulate the parallel-trading system on their own as well. Officials in Denmark, for example, inspect factories that are engaged in parallel trading to avert tampering with medicines.[18]

European officials also conduct enforcement activities. In March 2004, officials seized 500,000 dosage units of counterfeit medicines in Valencia, Spain. In addition to the tablets, officials found 1.2 million labels for use in the counterfeit operation. The drugs seized were for serious illnesses, such as HIV/AIDS and cancer.[19]

In the United Kingdom, the Medical and Healthcare Products Regulatory Agency relies on a voluntary reporting system called a "yellow card scheme" to respond to incidents of counterfeit and substandard drugs. The reporting system was instituted in the 1970s in response to the thalidomide disaster there.[20] Since the implementation of the system, over 400,000 cases have been reported, but further details are limited.[21]

Developing Countries. Aided by their relatively strong regulatory structures and enforcement agencies, developed countries have experienced significant success in stemming the flow of counterfeits into their markets. Developing countries, however, plagued by more pressing problems than fake drugs—including an utter lack of affordable drugs—have experienced less success. They often lack the regulatory power to monitor local counterfeit operations. Inefficiency and outright corruption in customs operations enable the importation of fakes from India, China, and elsewhere.

For developing nations, regulatory bodies are often an expensive and unaffordable luxury. According to WHO, only 20 percent of member states have well-developed drug regulation. Of the remaining members, only about 50 percent implement drug regulation at varying levels of development and operational capacity. The remaining 30 percent either have "no drug regulation in place or a very limited capacity that hardly functions."[22] Some of the more developed but poorly governed countries, such as Thailand, have national regulatory bodies, but these may be no more than money-making vehicles for political appointees.[23] In such cases, action may only be taken when pressure is put on a country by its neighbors or international bodies to remedy a domestic problem. Lacking adequate regulatory structures, countries must rely on action taken by international bodies for assessing and combating the fake drug problem. Indeed, these countries also rely on international organizations to fund most of their health care. Developing countries often lack data on the scope of their domestic counterfeit problems, making enforcement all the more difficult. But reform is possible with political will, as cases such as Nigeria illustrate.

Africa. Throughout the African continent, drug regulatory authorities vary in size and scope; anticounterfeiting legislation, where it exists, may be imperfectly enforced. A lack of rigorous, representative data collection in many countries makes it difficult even to assess accurately the scope of the problem.[24]

Nigeria, as one of the richer countries in sub-Saharan Africa, was for many years the chief market for counterfeit drugs. In 2002, Nigerian health officials estimated that counterfeits made up approximately 40 percent of the drug market there.[25] At one point, a study put the estimate of fake antimalarials in Nigeria at 85 percent of the total market.[26]

Nigeria's regulatory body, the National Agency for Food and Drug Administration and Control (NAFDAC), was established in 1993, but for years it was largely ineffective in controlling the production and distribution of fake drugs. Political support for NAFDAC was weak. Not until several neighboring countries, including Ghana and Sierra Leone, banned all pharmaceutical products made in Nigeria did leaders in Abuja take action. In 2000, then-president Olusegun Obasanjo dismissed the management of NAFDAC. In 2001, he appointed Dora Akunyili to run it.[27] She reorganized the agency with Obasanjo's full political support and strengthened import and export security. The importation of drugs and other regulated products through land borders was banned outright, and limited to two seaports (Calabar in the eastern part of the country and Apapa in

Lagos, the country's most populous city in the southwestern part of the country) and two airports (Murtala Mohammed International in Lagos and Mallam Aminu Kano International in the north). NAFDAC was also given the authority to demand that the Nigerian Ports Authority, independent shipping lines, and airlines release shipping and cargo manifests to agency inspectors.

Between 2001 and 2006, Nigerian officials destroyed more than $109 million worth of fake drugs.[28] In 2006, officials estimated that counterfeits made up approximately 16 percent of the total market, down from a high of anywhere between 40 and 85 percent.[29] That year, NAFDAC created the West African Drug Regulatory Authorities Network, a forum for West African drug regulators to strategize on combating counterfeit operations in the region.[30]

Authorities appeared to be growing more adept at the complex coordination required to identify and shut down counterfeit operations. In March 2007, after seven months of planning and coordination by different Nigerian agencies, NAFDAC closed down the notorious Onitsha Bridge Head Market.[31] Just a year earlier, NAFDAC officials surveying the market had been attacked and driven out by counterfeiters operating inside it; twelve Nigerian policemen had fled the scene, and six of their vehicles had been smashed.

In many African countries, inefficiency and outright corruption at the borders tend to enable the importation of fake drugs, often from India and China.[32] Some importers dupe customs agents into believing their products are safe and legal. They may, for instance, hide their fake drugs inside containers with other goods, like clothing or household items, or simply declare them to regulators as other items.[33] Most often, however, counterfeiters capitalize on border corruption.[34] According to Akunyili, "The first line of action by drug counterfeiters is to compromise regulators. When this fails, they fight back with intimidation, harassment, blackmail, and threats."[35] Counterfeiters are able to "compromise regulators" by bribing them to maintain lax regulations; they are able to compromise customs officials by bribing them to overlook certain packages. Regulators and customs officials reluctant to play along will be threatened until they acquiesce or leave their jobs. In 2003, Akunyili herself was the target of an assassination attempt. A bullet grazed her head in a drive-by shooting. She has admirably affirmed her commitment to the anti-fake cause, but such menacing tactics are likely to frighten weaker personnel working in the supply chain.

Other countries, such as Uganda, have also moved to strengthen internal production standards. According to U.S. Pharmacopeia, Uganda's National Drug Authority carries out mandatory, batch-by-batch laboratory analysis of all medicines intended to treat malaria and tuberculosis before they are cleared for entry into the country.[36] Still, the relatively low number of regulatory personnel in Uganda (WHO reports that there were only three to four per one million people in 1998, the lowest number out of the ten countries surveyed) suggests that implementation may be far from perfect.[37]

Indeed, weak health infrastructures and a lack of adequately trained regulatory personnel often stymie the rigorous implementation of anticounterfeiting initiatives in Africa. Zimbabwe, for example, appears on paper to have a robust drug regulation system. The main functions of its core institution, the Medicines Control Authority of Zimbabwe (MCAZ), include "licensing of manufacturing, product assessment and registration, GMP inspection, import controls and control of product quality,"[38] as well as maintaining controls over prescription of medication, licensing requirements for the wholesale trade of drugs, and the inspection of drug distribution and promotion channels.[39] Still, economic instability[40] and the country's weak national health infrastructure mean that this regulatory legislation has not been well enforced—and that it has done little to combat counterfeiting.[41] One problem is a lack of personnel; one study estimated that in 2002, 27 percent of staff posts at the MCAZ were vacant, and that the agency had only four staffers per million Zimbabweans.[42]

In July 2007, the MCAZ issued an official statement about the high levels of fake ARVs that were available in Zimbabwe. According to officials, unlicensed individuals were selling "counterfeited, adulterated and contaminated" drugs in local markets and salons; the market for unauthorized drugs in the country could run into the billions of dollars.[43]

In Kenya, the situation is similar: Although drug regulatory legislation exists, poor enforcement and a shortage of well-trained regulatory staff render it ineffective. Kenya's Drug Inspectorate Unit, for example, has just ten inspectors for the entire country.[44] The Pharmaceutical Inspectorate Unit at the Pharmacy and Poisons Board has only five staff members (all pharmacists); the board itself has only seven members.[45] Tasked with carrying out inspection, regulation, and quality-control functions, these board members tend to be desperately overcommitted.[46]

A lack of health facilities and the high cost of drugs also lead many people to self-prescribe, relying on *dukas* (kiosks) for their supplies of paracetamol, antimalarials, anti-inflammatories, and antibiotics.[47] Buying from *dukas* circumvents the regulatory structure, however weak it may be, making the population even more susceptible to counterfeit drugs.

Given the lack of regulatory enforcement and a thriving informal sector, it is not surprising that counterfeits have infiltrated the system at an alarming rate. The Kenyan Association of Pharmaceutical Industry estimates that $130 million worth of counterfeit pharmaceuticals are sold in the country annually.[48] WHO estimates that 30 percent of drugs on the market in Kenya are counterfeit,[49] and some local sources place the proportion much higher, between 50 and 70 percent.[50]

According to Hezekiah Chepkwony, director of the National Quality Control Laboratory for Drugs and Medical Devices, reform is needed. "We recently received bulk raw materials of Amoxicillin Trihydrate and Ampicillin Trihydrate that had no active ingredients at all, yet these are some of the highly used [sic] antibiotics in Kenya," Chepkwony told the *Kenya Standard* in August 2005. According to Chepkwony, political commitment must be strengthened, legislation revised, and national drug control authorities adequately funded and empowered. More training needs to be provided for law enforcement and customs personnel, and the Kenyan government needs to work with the international community to stem the flow of counterfeit drugs into the country.[51]

Latin America. In Latin America, anticounterfeiting initiatives at the regional level have been led by the Pan American Health Organization and two of its subsidiaries, the Pan American Network for Drug Regulatory Harmonization (PANDRH) and the Pharmaceutical Forum of the Americas.[52] PANDRH exists to "promote drug regulatory harmonization for all aspects of quality, safety and efficacy of pharmaceutical products" in all member countries, coordinating initiatives and sharing knowledge among member states.[53] This is no small task; regulatory structures remain diverse and highly fragmented, and WHO reports that Latin America is "lagging behind" other regions in regulatory coordination.[54]

In Peru, for example, a national drug authority exists within the Ministry of Health (the Dirección General de Medicamentos, Insumos y Drogas)[55] but is struggling to control the production, importation, and distribution of counterfeit pharmaceuticals. WHO estimates that around two hundred pharmacies operate in downtown Lima with neither registration nor authorization from the Ministry of Health.[56] In Venezuela, "strict controls" and "clear norms and procedures," coupled with the use of a computerized drug regulation system, have made regulation more effective. Even so, as a WHO study indicates, staff shortages and a lack of financing have rendered implementation imperfect.[57]

When its interests are at stake, the United States facilitates the transfer of expertise to Latin America. Because of its geographical proximity and trade importance to the United States, Mexico has enjoyed special attention from the FDA and the U.S. Department of Health and Human Services.[58] On the enforcement side, Interpol launched Project Jupiter in the Americas, which was praised by the 2005 Second Global Conference on Global Counterfeiting (involving five hundred delegates from sixty-six countries) as a model for effective transnational enforcement operations.[59]

Russia. The Russian government has recently stepped up action against counterfeiters and is even challenging the bureaucratic corruption that has allowed the trade to thrive there. In 2007, police and inspectors from the Russian Federal Agency for Monitoring Health and Social Development (Roszdravnadzor) raided a run-down Moscow warehouse and found an estimated two million dollars' worth of copies of popular, mostly foreign-produced drugs such as vinpocetine (branded as Cavinton, a drug used for the treatment of various cerebral insufficiency conditions), the cold remedy TeraFlu, and the antibacterial co-trimoxazole.

According to Ramil Khabriev, the former head of Roszdravnadzor, rapid progress is being made. All drugs entering the country are certified, and a new law enacted in June 2007 has made it possible to take distributors and pharmacies—which are often in on the sale of counterfeits—to arbitration court and annul their licenses. Khabriev says that "the number of inspections has increased while at the same time the quantity of counterfeits being found has decreased." This suggests that such efforts have been successful.[60] While Gennady Shirshov of Russia's Union of Professional Pharmaceutical Organizations welcomes the government action that has closed down the biggest manufacturers of fakes, he fears that smaller producers making lower-quality counterfeits will move in to fill the void. Law enforcement bodies are ill-equipped, and legislation inadequate, to provide a deterrent.[61]

Meanwhile, Roszdravnadzor is considering introducing a system of coded labels to identify legitimate drugs, and Intertech Corporation in Moscow has developed a tool for the SPFO, using near-infrared technology—common elsewhere in Europe—that can identify counterfeit drugs and packaging within minutes. The suitcase-sized device, which is linked to a personal computer, can test liquids, powders, and receptacles for the content of ampoules and pills. The SPFO wants to set up a database of profiles of legitimate medicines to compare with suspected copycats.

But Sergei Boboshko of the Moscow-based Association of International Pharmaceutical Manufacturers casts doubt on the efficacy of security devices: "There are no stamps, no holograms, no secret passwords, or anything that's going to eradicate this problem."[62]

Asia. In May 2007, China announced that Zheng Xiaoyu, the former head of the State Food and Drug Agency (SFDA), had been sentenced to death after being found guilty of taking bribes from eight pharmaceutical and medical equipment firms and illegally approving their products.[63] Zheng's sentence followed a series of medical scandals that killed dozens in China and undermined national and international confidence in the country's fast-developing pharmaceutical industry, which may have reduced the volume of drugs exported from the country.[64]

The harsh sentence was intended to be a warning. After all, such bribery had been business as usual, and many other officials had accepted larger payments and received lighter sentences. Wang Yuexing, board secretary of the SFDA, promised that his officials would be more disciplined in processing new drug applications, to the benefit of law-abiding pharmaceutical firms.[65] As of late 2007, this new approach appeared to be paying dividends: In December, the deputy head of China's Food and Drug Administration, Wu Zhen, announced that pharmaceutical companies had withdrawn more than 7,300 applications for drug registrations, approximately 24 percent of the total.[66]

The Chinese government has also moved to make licensing requirements for drug manufacturers more rigorous. Since the July 2007 launch of a nationwide campaign to crack down on counterfeiting, more than three hundred drug and medical-device manufacturers have been shut down for poor-quality products.[67] Effective in 2008, the Chinese government will not grant licenses to pharmaceutical companies with any "severe defects" in their drug manufacturing processes, including the submission of false information. The rules previously had permitted a producer to obtain a license if three defects were found but corrected.[68] Evidence suggests that pharmaceutical companies in the country are taking the government seriously.

Still, more reforms are necessary. As noted in the U.S. Trade Representative's 2007 annual report on the state of international intellectual property rights, China still possesses "safe harbors," or unduly high thresholds for criminal liability. Because the minimum value of counterfeited products required to initiate criminal prosecution—normally calculated on the basis of the price the counterfeited product can fetch in the market—is prohibitively high in China, published penalties can be little more than straw-man threats.[69] If only one counterfeit product is discovered, the manufacturer can only be prosecuted based upon the price of that single product. In a move to correct this problem, the SFDA announced in November 2007 that it plans to impose stiffer penalties (including heavy fines, life imprisonment, and the death penalty) in counterfeit-drug cases that lead to "very serious damage," regardless of the value of drugs involved. Defined as "serious deformities," "grievous bodily harm" to more than three people, or "slight injury" to more than ten, "very serious damage" expands the number of cases in which counterfeiters can be held liable.[70]

Even with such reforms, China will likely face significant logistical and social challenges in cracking down on counterfeit production. The number of drug wholesalers in China has burgeoned, bloated in part by the dismantling of the state-run, state-funded public health system that began in the late 1970s. Released from government pensions, the "barefoot doctors" have embraced the selling of drugs as lucrative new employment.[71] Sales of counterfeits are ostentatious; as the *Wall Street Journal* has noted, fake Viagra tablets can be bought in Chinese airport lounges.[72]

As discussed earlier, the other major Asian source of counterfeit drugs is India. There we find that progress has been inhibited by bureaucratic disagreement about the extent of the problem.[73] Without a clear consensus on the prevalence of fakes in its domestic drug market—existing estimates range from 3 to 30 percent,[74] with the official estimate at less than 1 percent[75]—lawmakers have been slow to reform India's weak regulatory system.

Anticounterfeiting initiatives have also been hampered by the country's penal code,[76] which has emphasized the illegality of trafficking in narcotics but not the counterfeiting of patented drugs. Although many private pharmaceutical companies, concerned with protecting their brands, have conducted raids confiscating counter-feit drugs, these raids have tended to result in little punitive action. Only drugs deemed to be "narcotics" under the Narcotic Drugs and Psychotropic Substances Act (NDPSA) of 1985 were considered worthy of investigation by India's Criminal Bureau of Investigations (CBI). The faking of nonnarcotics was a local matter unworthy of federal action.[77] The latest drug law in India, a 2007 amendment to the NDPSA rules, may improve matters.[78]

Drug laws in many other Southeast Asian nations are similarly inadequate to prevent the penetration of fakes across borders. As a recent editorial in Thailand's *Bangkok Post* lamented, "Our present drug law is more than forty years old and too outdated to deal with e-commerce and counterfeit pharmaceuticals being shepherded across borders."[79]

In India, as elsewhere, inadequate regulation has been further constrained by government bureaucracy and the lack of facilities and trained personnel. As of 2003, at least eleven out of India's twenty-eight states did not have any laboratories for testing drugs, and in the remaining seventeen states with functioning labs, only seven were adequately equipped, according to Raghunath Mashelkar, former director general of India's Council of Scientific and Industrial Research.[80] Enforcement against counterfeiters remains weak; the *Hindustan Times* reported in July 2007 that counterfeit-drug manufacturers were able to forge documents that allowed them to sell fakes to government-run hospitals at a hand-some profit.[81]

Until recently, illegitimate drug producers in India also benefited from the country's patent system. For years India granted only *process* patents instead of the *product* patents approved by the Organisation for Economic Co-operation and Development (OECD) governments. A process patent protected the process that the drug company in question used to create a new drug, but not the end product of that process. Therefore, any company that could reverse-engineer a Western product and was able to produce the same drug using a slightly different process could do so freely, thus under-cutting the sale of the original, protected drug. This opened the door for numerous generic producers to enter the market, and, with so many small firms legitimately supplying it, cover was provided to fakers. Beginning in 2005, this system was reformed, and India began granting product patents, making it harder for counterfeiters to enter the system.[82]

More reforms are planned in India. The Indian Central Drugs Standard Control Organization, which is a part of the Ministry of Health and Family Welfare, has intended to "intensify surveillance of high risk areas," such as marketplaces, border zones, and rural areas, as well as implement rapid-alert mechanisms.[83] The country recently said it would conduct a nationwide survey of the presence of fake drugs in the market.[84]

On the enforcement side, India has demonstrated some willingness to convict and punish counterfeiters. In January 2008, a court in Thane sentenced a man found guilty of manufacturing spurious medicines to fifteen years in prison and a fine equivalent to $13,400.[85] Perhaps most promisingly, Indian health minister Anbumani Ramadoss announced, also in January 2008, that the government planned to set up a central drug authority modeled after and drawing on the technical expertise of the U.S. Food and Drug Administration. The agency, however, will take six to seven years to be completely operational.[86]

A problem that has become particularly acute in Southeast Asia is the distribution of counterfeit antimalarials. One study estimates that between 38 and 52 percent of blister packs labeled as artesunate, a powerful antimalarial, contain no active ingredient.[87] Increasingly, artesunate drugs that contain some active ingredient (but in insufficient quantities to kill the parasite) are emerging on shelves in kiosks and pharmacies. In Burma, for example, counterfeit artesunate samples collected in 2006 were found to have between 3.5 and 12.1 mg of artesunate per tablet, less than one-fifth the amount in a standard, authentic tablet. Such counterfeits have not only caused grievous loss of life, as sick individuals who would have otherwise obtained authentic medicines effectively went untreated; they have also made the parasite more resistant to the once-effective drug. They have led to a loss of confidence in artesunate-based medicines and in some cases have expanded artemisinin resistance.[88] As in Africa, the problem is exacerbated by poverty; authentic artesunate and artesunate combination therapies (ACTs) can be expensive, and consumers often opt for less expensive alternatives, even when their quality is suspect. One approach to solving this problem would be to flood the market with good-quality drugs, such as with the proposal to offer a global subsidy for ACTs. Many uncertainties with this proposal exist, however; the cost may be prohibitive, and the subsidy may not work properly.[89]

Some countries in Southeast Asia are beginning to take measures to combat the problem of counterfeit drugs by working to equip consumers and pharmacists with a means to differentiate authentic from fake products. In 2005, Malaysia introduced its Meditag program, which required all products registered with the Malaysian Drug Control Authority to bear a holographic security device, marketed by Mediharta and affixed by one of the company's labeling contractors. In 2006, the program expanded by supplying pharmacies with decoder units designed to be placed on store counters or shelves with instructions on their use. Pharmacists and even consumers are encouraged to check the authenticity of a given medicine's Meditag by sliding the medicine pack under the decoder unit. Consumers are also encouraged to verify the registration numbers of the medicines by checking with the pharmacy enforcement branch of the ministry or by visiting its website.[90] In addition to enabling consumers to police their own purchases, Meditag has buttressed local law enforcement. Some of Malaysia's three hundred roving enforcement officers are equipped with portable readers.

Although it is difficult to be certain, given a paucity of data and other influences,[91] it appears that the Meditag program has had at least some positive effects. As of June 2007, RM 13.77 million ($4.05 million) in unregistered medicines and cosmetics had been seized, up from RM 7.83 million ($2.3 million) for all of 2006 (including, in the latter case, RM 5.8 million, worth $1.7 million, of unregistered medicines).[92] At least some countries have shown an interest in adopting the Malaysian model. In August 2007, Nigeria's NAFDAC announced plans to introduce uniquely numbered holographic labels to be used on all licensed medicines distributed in the country.[93]

Throughout the world, governments now realize the danger to public health of substandard medicines—whether they are counterfeits or just poor-quality products from legitimate companies—and are more willing to take action. Countries that had grown infamous for flooding the world with fakes now recognize the problems caused by illegal production—damage to the health of the home population and loss of reputation in the world markets—and are working to shut it down. As has been demonstrated in Nigeria, the will to take action is the most significant factor in maintaining a safe drug supply.

Unilateral Private Action

The private sector has powerful incentives to stem the deluge of fakes from illicit producers into international supply chains. Patent-holding pharmaceutical companies find their reputations tarnished and their profit margins pinched when fakes masquerading as their trademarked products are recalled or when consumers stop buying safe products because they are not sure they are getting the real thing.

Independent Organizations. U.S. Pharmacopeia and its European counterpart (European Pharmacopeia) are helping middle-income and poor countries ensure the quality of their medicines. The USP provides a handbook of basic requirements for a medicine regulatory agency, with step-by-step instructions for providing those services, including the evaluation and registration of medicinal products and the inspection and licensing of manufacturing premises, import and export agents, distributors, wholesalers, and retail outlets.[94]

Also providing assistance is the Pharmaceutical Research and Manufacturers of America (PhRMA)—the pharmaceutical industry's advocacy group—which has established a website to help educate consumers on the dangers of counterfeit drugs.[95] In Asia, the Japan Pharmaceutical Manufacturers Association (JPMA) has spearheaded efforts to improve quality-control training and identification of counterfeits. It has donated to Laos and Cambodia high-performance liquid chromatography systems to assess the chemical makeup of pharmaceutical drugs and thereby identify potential counterfeits. It has also conducted training in quality-control measures for Asian regulatory personnel. In 2006, the organization initiated the JPMA/Ministry of Health project in collaboration with the Cambodian Department of Drugs and Food, designed to measure the effectiveness of various anticounterfeiting programs. JPMA has also promoted the Counterfeit Drug Survey Project, an international cooperative enterprise in Asia.[96]

Some individual drug companies have voluntarily initiated sample testing of drugs being imported into the United States to ensure the security of the U.S. supply chain. The USP sets standards for drug quality that it makes available to drug manufacturers, and provides a quality-testing service for firms that, by independently verifying the quality of drugs and the integrity of the production process, serves a valuable credentialing function for consumers at both the manufacturing and wholesale levels. Producers who voluntarily agree to the USP's testing are subjected to an initial audit that checks for compliance with internationally accepted good manufacturing practice guidelines,[97] as well as a thorough documentation review and a battery of laboratory tests checking their drugs for purity and potency. Firms that pass receive a USP Verified Mark and are subject to biennial reviews.[98]

The Pharmaceutical Security Initiative (PSI), a consortium of twenty-one manufacturers from several different countries, aggregates data on counterfeit drugs from participating drug companies and provides them with a broad picture of the counterfeit industry. PSI also has an incident-based reporting system through which pharmaceutical companies can report cases of counterfeit drugs entering supply chains, thus keeping participating members abreast of all relevant counterfeiting cases.

The Global Pharma Health Fund (GPHF) is a public-private partnership of the German government and pharmaceutical companies that has developed an effective anticounterfeiting measure which it calls a "minilab." The minilab is a mobile device that health providers can use to quickly and easily test the efficacy of over forty types of the drugs they receive, including important antimalarials, antibiotics, and ARVs. The GPHF sells its minilabs at relatively low prices (averaging $6,000) to health providers around the world,[99] but especially in Africa and Southeast Asia. As of July 2007, it had sold over 240 minilabs in sixty-five countries.[100]

Pharmaceutical Companies. Individual pharmaceutical firms have also taken steps to resist counterfeit drugs. Many have begun to implement track-and-trace technology on their drugs to provide an effective "e-pedigree" to distributors and consumers. Some have experimented with using radio frequency identification (RFID) technology to check the e-pedigrees of drug shipments, although, in the United States, this is not yet required by the FDA.[101]

To help secure the complex, vulnerable global supply chain, many drug companies have implemented their own security measures. Pfizer announced in December 2003 that all distributors in the United States selling its products would have to purchase them directly from the company or from selected wholesalers.[102] In September 2006, Pfizer announced that it would cease selling drugs to eighteen wholesalers in the United Kingdom and instead distribute drugs there only through UniChem.[103] These moves are attempts to cut down the size of the secondary wholesale market, which includes sales among wholesalers.[104]

Other pharmaceutical firms will need to secure their own supply chains and alert the public when they become aware of counterfeit drugs. These companies already recall all affected drugs, and, increasingly, they are financing investigations and raids against counterfeiters worldwide. Companies cultivate relationships with local consultants—well-connected people who can find out where fake drugs are being produced and sold—who provide evidence to local police, who then raid the sites identified. In India, for example, Suresh Sati, who markets himself as "The Protector," is a private investigator who has carried out raids on behalf of many companies. Still, it is important to note that such raids will only be successful when they are backed by a regulatory commitment to prosecute and punish counterfeiters. As discussed earlier in this section, the reluctance of India's Criminal Bureau of Investigations means that raids by private companies in India have had only limited deterrence power.[105]

Pharmacists. Pharmacists have a lot to lose from poor-quality drugs. Being trusted by one's customers is important for retailers, especially when the average consumer cannot ascertain whether the product is genuine or fake, and the product's quality can mean the difference between life and death. Most pharmacists, especially in the developed world, assume that the supply chain is secure, and they rely on alerts from their suppliers or the FDA to inform them otherwise.[106] They also may be well-trained in spotting substandard medicines (pills that appear degraded; packaging that appears suspect or is the wrong color, size, or shape). But sometimes even skilled practitioners depend on luck. Fake Viagra was once unearthed by the FDA because the packaging was slightly larger than it should have been—a discovery that was made when the dispenser could not shut the desk drawer where he kept his Viagra supplies.[107]

As the proliferation of fakes into even legitimate supply chains increases, luck may not be enough. In the developing world, where regulatory structures remain weak and supply chains cannot always be easily secured, pharmacists represent an important front line of defense.

Overall, private sector action, whether by independent organizations, consortia of pharmaceutical companies, individual companies, or pharmacists, provides an important, bottom-up complement to government policy. By demonstrating a commitment to the integrity of their own supply and distribution chains, private companies and pharmacists instill trust in and promote demand for high-quality products. By sharing information with government regulatory agencies and enforcement agents, the private sector can also improve the efficiency of the public sector in combating the counterfeit trade.

4

Policy Recommendations

Counterfeiters do not operate in a vacuum. Impelled by unscrupulous criminals but enabled by weak regulatory structures and uninformed or unconcerned consumers, the counterfeit problem has thrived under the prevailing policy framework. Although there are no cure-all pills for the fake-drug disease, several policy changes can create a new framework that will mitigate the problem instead of enable it.

At the International Level

International aid agencies can effectively fight counterfeiting, often by simply not contributing to its spread. As countries negotiate trade deals among themselves, they should pursue free trade without protectionist barriers, but with protection for intellectual property. In Europe, the parallel-trading system ought to be reassessed in light of the opportunities it affords counterfeiters. The following steps will contribute to such efforts:

Donor agencies must ensure that they are not purchasing or distributing substandard or counterfeit medicines. Many drugs distributed in the developing world—especially those for HIV/AIDS and malaria—are donated (or sold at bargain-basement prices) by aid agencies, many of which have demonstrated little regard for ensuring the quality of drugs they purchase and distribute. The Global Fund to Fight AIDS, Tuberculosis and Malaria, for example, a procurement agency responsible for allocating about $4.7 billion for health interventions consisting primarily of essential drugs, has spent millions on medicines of uncertain quality. In one round of drug procurement, 56 percent of purchase orders (five of nine) made by the Global Fund went to suppliers approved neither by WHO nor another more stringent agency.[1] In its bid to encourage small producers in developing countries, the Global Fund has included several untested copies of drugs on its prequalification list that may or may not be bio-equivalent to their branded counterparts; as of June 2007, only 7 percent of antimalarials on the Global Fund's list had under-gone testing to demonstrate bioequivalence to a branded original. On October 10, 2007, the Global Fund quietly removed twenty-two previously approved antimalarial formulations from its compliance list. Although the formulation of six of the remaining eight is still not approved by a stringent regulatory agency—and only approved by the historically unreliable WHO prequalification process—this is a major step forward. But more needs to be done.[2] In 2004, the FDA offered free, fast-track bioequivalence testing for HIV/AIDS antiretrovirals on WHO's prequalification list after the list had rightly been criticized for including eighteen anti-HIV drugs that had not demonstrated bioequivalence. Today, the FDA might consider doing something similar for the Global Fund and other aid agencies engaging in unsound drug distribution practices.[3] International organizations might consider setting up testing laboratories for particular regions. This would enable the more efficient testing of locally produced drugs.

Aid agencies should pair drug distribution with educational initiatives on the proper use, storage, and prescription of drugs, especially antimalarials. Distributors in the developing world should be educated on the danger posed by counterfeits, trained to identify fakes in the market, and equipped with tools to facilitate such identification. Although sophisticated technology may not be available or financially feasible in all places, relatively inexpensive and easy-to-use tools, such as the GPHF minilab, could be more broadly used.[4]

At the National Level

National regulatory agencies can be powerful outlets for anticounter-feiting reforms. They should insist on more streamlined and trans-parent supply chains and adopt stricter licensure requirements for middlemen between manufacturers and consumers. Such reforms will be futile, however, unless the regulators are independent, uncompromising, and courageous.

Developing countries should lower tariffs on imports and embrace free trade with patent protection. By lowering tariffs on imported lifesaving medicines, developing countries can cut prices and offer greater access to medicines for their citizens.[5] This is a dif-ficult policy to embrace for any country suffering from a lack of con-fidence in its economy. While some might argue that lowering tariffs reduces an important source of government revenue—and thereby government services, including in the health care sector—the empir-ical record suggests the opposite.[6] Indeed, developed countries still cling to such protectionist policies to protect sectors of their economies against foreign competition. However, taxes and tariffs do little to increase government spending on health services; consumers may see prices increase by up to 100 percent with no appreciable impact on government health care spending.[7] In fact, complex tariff and tax structures create ready entry points for corruption, smug-gling, and counterfeiting, stimulating "demand for cheaper fakes by artificially driving up the price of legitimate drugs through taxes and tariffs which further inflate the retail price of the drugs," accord-ing to the International Policy Network.[8] India and Nigeria are apt examples: Both levy extremely high tariff rates on imported drugs, and both suffer from weak health infrastructures and insufficient access to high-quality medicines. The high price and scarcity of imported products, and the lack of regulation in the health-care sector, create conditions under which distributors, retailers, and consumers are willing to buy cut-price products. Inevitably, demand for high-quality products will be reduced, which allows fake or substandard products into the market.

High tariffs also discourage legitimate international suppliers from doing business in poor countries. Drug exporters complain repeatedly that customs fees in Ethiopia—where less than 20 percent of the population has access to medical care—are too high for drugs that have only a limited market in the country, which forces companies to consider not selling products that may not generate sufficient sales. To make matters worse, strict documentation requirements and demands for the payment of "small" fees—supposedly for customs "support" services—are bound to make exporters wary. In cases in which companies practice differential pricing, whereby drugs are sold at a considerably smaller profit margin in developing countries than in the developed world, tariff hassles may simply prompt drug companies to move their business elsewhere.[9]

Many countries have been reluctant to eliminate tariffs because they generate revenue from Western companies—a reliable source compared to domestic companies. Some, notably India, Kenya, Thailand, and Brazil, use tariffs to protect domestic drug industries, while others, such as Vietnam, Tanzania, and Ethiopia, may maintain tariffs to assist development of domestic pharmaceutical industries. This makes little economic sense. While a few developing countries, such as India and Brazil, have thriving local drug industries, most lack the requisite pharmaceutical manufacturing capacity and are dependent on imports or the benevolence of philanthropic organizations for their supplies. Protecting local industries from international competition does not necessarily guarantee that sustainable companies will emerge to meet consumer demand internationally and generate long-run income.

In addition to lowering tariffs, countries should actively work to secure intellectual property rights and protect patents. Although pharmaceutical patents have been heavily criticized as an impediment to drug access in the developing world, they serve an important role in guaranteeing long-term drug development. Researching a drug involves high fixed costs and significant risk; in the United States, research and development amounts to almost 20 percent of the research-based pharmaceutical industry's total global sales every year.[10] Patent protection coupled with differential pricing would strike the middle ground between promoting short-term access and guaranteeing long-term supply. Countries that choose to disregard patents may find their supply of front-line drugs compromised, as demonstrated by drug manufacturer Abbott's exodus from Thailand.[11]

Protection of patents creates an environment in which legitimate manufacturers have a reason to expose competitors whose products are poorly formulated. By promoting innovation—not merely off-branding—developing countries also may establish a sustainable niche for themselves in pharmaceutical manufacturing. Two current examples are the leading Indian drug firms, Ranbaxy and Cipla. Ranbaxy is developing a new and patentable dosage form of Bayer's antibiotic Ciprobay (ciprofloxacin) before the patent expires, while Cipla has developed a new-dosage form of AstraZeneca's anti-ulcer drug, Losec. At the same time, Indian drug companies are also developing new molecules.[12]

Developed countries can encourage the protection of intellectual property rights by promoting only limited use of the compulsory licenses under Trade Related Aspects of Intellectual Property Agreements (TRIPS), part of the World Trade Organization's Doha negotiations. As amended in 2005, TRIPS allow member countries to issue compulsory licenses enabling domestic industry or third parties to manufacture drugs off-patent legally. Although designed to be used only in cases of "national emergency or other circumstances of extreme urgency," generally pertaining to public health,[13] TRIPS exceptions have been overused. In January 2007, for example, Thailand issued a compulsory license for Plavix, a blood-thinning treatment to help prevent heart disease.[14]

To address such abuses, the U.S. Trade Representative can consider acting under "special 301" provisions of the Trade Act of 1974, placing countries on a "priority watch list" to call attention to their disregard for intellectual property rights, as it did in 2007 with Thailand.[15] The priority watch list can be an effective tool in calling attention to—and encouraging the correction of—a country's violations of intellectual property rights. In 2006, for instance, the U.S. Trade Representative announced it was removing the Philippines from its priority watch list following improvements in the country's legislation and enforcement against counterfeit production.[16] According to the director general of the Intellectual Property Office of the Philippines, Adrian S. Cristobal Jr., the islands' "end goal" is to make further improvements, culminating in the removal of the country from the U.S. secondary watch list.[17]

If they fail to protect intellectual property rights, developing countries may find themselves without a reliable supply of high-quality, lifesaving drugs, as Western companies may choose simply to cease distribution in a country that does not protect property rights.[18]

Western countries should reevaluate European Union parallel trade. Some theorists have argued that parallel trade in pharmaceuticals is an effective form of arbitrage, leading to more efficient market operation;[19] others argue that it destroys efficient differential pricing and provides opportunities for counterfeiters to insert fakes into the system.[20] Parallel traders defend their system by suggesting that they help identify fakes in the market. As Tomasz Dzitko, president and CEO of Polish wholesaler Delpharma, asserted in a presentation at a 2007 conference on parallel trade, it is not unknown for parallel traders to detect defects in products and report them to the manufacturers and regulatory authorities concerned.[21] A 2004 study by the London School of Economics and Political Science, however, found that the vast majority of benefits from parallel trade accrued directly to parallel importers, with "zero, or at best marginal benefits to patients."[22] The study, said author Panos Kanavos, prescribed "urgent further debate before any additional legislation in support of parallel trade is passed . . . There is no evidence of sustainable dynamic price competition in destination countries, with no corresponding indirect cost savings."[23] Similarly, in her review of drug prices and sales from 1993 to 2004 in the European Union, economist Margaret Kyle found that parallel importing had done little to reduce prices of drugs, as pharmaceutical firms moved to differentiate their products across countries through unique packaging and version requirements.[24]

In short, EU parallel trading certainly increases the possibility for fake insertion, possibly increases the fake trade, and potentially undermines economic efficiency. The United States should not undertake any parallel trading (as has been suggested by various legislators)[25] without an independent analysis of the EU system. Given the potential harms from parallel trading, the European Union might want to rein it in.

Public and private actors should collaborate on appropriate technology to create a transparent and verifiable chain of custody from the point of production to the point of sale. As recommended by the FDA's Counterfeit Task Force (a group created in 2003 to offer advice to policymakers about the growing threat posed by counterfeit and substandard drugs) and mandated in the 2007 Food and Drug Administration Amendments Act,[26] pharmaceutical companies, wholesalers, and pharmacies should collaborate to design and implement a nationwide serialization system with track-and-trace technology for all drugs produced in the United States.[27]

The "e-pedigree" has been piloted in several states (including California, which requires that all drugs be included under the system by January 2009), but it has not been adopted on a national scale, which has made tracing drugs across state borders—and across different credentialing systems and pedigree requirements—prohibitive.[28]

Numerous technologies can ensure this e-pedigree is not compromised by counterfeiters. Radio frequency identification appears especially promising. An RFID tag, applied to a shipment of pharmaceuticals, can be read from several feet away using radio waves. In the United States, RFID may prove especially helpful in speeding the passage of drugs through customs, where thousands of drug packages become backlogged every year. Such backlogs can create perverse incentives for customs officials to push shipments through, even if they suspect they may be counterfeit. They have also enabled "return to sender" policies, in which suspected counterfeit shipments are merely returned to the wholesaler, which can then redistribute them back through the system.[29] Several private pharmaceutical companies have experimented with RFID in their supply chains, but they are keeping tight-lipped about its relative cost-effectiveness.[30] More research must be conducted to determine the best-suited and most cost-effective technologies for tracking drug shipments.

In Europe, the European Medicines Agency should consider instituting a bar code requirement for drugs that are parallel-traded. In its most recent strategy report, the agency noted that while "enforcement of medicines legislation is the competency of Member States," increased coordination among various national and international bodies is essential—and lacking.[31] A bar code system would operate as a guardian of information, rather than an enforcement agent, facilitating coordination among EU member states without infringing on individual countries' mandates.

Under this system, all drug packages would be required to include a unique barcode on their original packaging, authenticating when, where, and by whom the drug was produced. Scanned at every border and—ideally—at every transaction between wholesalers, this barcode could then be tracked by pharmacies and law enforcement officials. In order to prevent the swapping of barcodes among shipments (which might be done to mask their origins), original packaging would, in all cases, need to be retained, which is impossible under current parallel-trading arrangements.

Governments should support a secure supply chain by taking measures to ensure post-production drug safety. Securing the supply chain includes making applications for drug wholesaler licenses more rigorous and increasing penalties—and enforcement power to impose these penalties—for counterfeiters. Communication channels among enforcement agencies—which in the United States are the FDA, the DEA, and customs—must also be streamlined. While many developing countries lack the regulatory structures and technical capacity for sophisticated supply-chain management and post-production drug safety schemes, reforms of the FDA and other national drug authorities in developed countries serve as models.

Particularly in developed countries, policymakers should work to correct the worrisome asymmetry between the resources expended to ensure the safety of a drug before it is approved for distribution and those used to guarantee its quality after it goes to market. In the United States, before a drug is approved for the general public, it must undergo a battery of tests coordinated by the FDA, primarily under the auspices of the Office of New Drugs (OND). The process is both long and expensive, perhaps as it should be.[32] Once a product reaches the market, however, the resources available for ensuring its quality decrease dramatically. The Office of Drug Safety (ODS), the primary office within the FDA charged with evaluating and monitoring post-market drug safety, had expenditures of $26.9 million in 2005, less than one-fourth the amount allocated for the OND. The office had only 106 staff members, compared to the OND's 715, and it lacked independent decision-making power.[33] Not surprisingly, then, the FDA has had difficulty monitoring the commitments it and its pharmaceutical partners have made to conduct post-market studies designed to assess the ongoing quality of drugs in the market. As of September 2006, 71 percent of all post-market study commitments were still "pending."[34]

Strengthening post-production drug safety will include equipping customs agents and other law enforcement agencies with tools to identify and confiscate fakes before they enter the country, tasks important—and practically applicable—in developed and developing countries alike. As the Nigerian case discussed in chapters 1 and 3 suggests, rigorous controls from the top can significantly decrease the number of fakes able to penetrate a given market. In developed countries with complex regulatory structures, strengthening postproduction safety also includes clarifying and streamlining operations among the various agencies involved with regulating the process at the state and federal levels. According to Randall W. Lutter, acting associate commissioner for policy and planning at the FDA, an increase in counterfeit-drug seizures observed between 2003 and 2004 reflected not only

"increased awareness and vigilance at all levels of the drug distribution chain" but also "increased referrals from and coordination
with other state and federal law enforcement agencies and communication with drug manufacturers."[35]

The application process for wholesalers should be made more
rigorous, especially for smaller wholesalers who operate in local
niches. In the United States, the FDA could oversee and guarantee compliance with this process, with another body, perhaps
the independent National Association of Boards of Pharmacy
(NABP), providing certification protocols. While moving oversight and control from the state governments to the federal level
would be controversial, it might be warranted, given the interstate
trade in pharmaceuticals. Currently, differences in licensing systems among states complicate the federal government's efforts to
monitor compliance.[36] The effectiveness of the NABP's Verified-
Accredited Wholesale Distributors (VAWD) program, for example, in which wholesalers must undergo a compliance review,
licensure verification, inspection, background checks, and screen-
ing, has been hampered by the fact that it is voluntary in most
states. (Only Indiana requires that all drug wholesalers receive
VAWD certification.) To date, only 224 wholesalers are VAWD-
certified—less than 4 percent of the approximately 6,500 currently operating in the United States. States have also been slow
to implement the FDA's 2005 recommendation to adopt NABP's
Model Rules for the Licensure of Wholesale Distributors.[37]

In other countries, governments can work with the FDA
and WHO to ensure that their own drug, manufacturer, and distributor registration programs are rigorous. Each country can
quickly learn from these authorities to distinguish between the
most important processes, which they should introduce first, and
the less vital ones that can be delayed until staffing and budgets
are larger.

Finally, criminal penalties for counterfeiting should be
increased to a level equal to those for trafficking in illicit drugs.
With higher penalties, the so-called narcotics crossovers—
syndicates and traders that have entered the counterfeit-drug

trade in recent years, impelled by high profits and comparatively low penalties—will have fewer incentives to continue operations. While they may simply reallocate some of their own resources back to narcotics trafficking—presenting another problem for policymakers—their impact on the health of unwitting consumers will be mitigated.

Increasing penalties for counterfeiting while simultaneously decreasing the total number of counterfeiters may have the unintended effect of making those that remain more organized and violent. Leaving fewer counterfeiters in the market will, however, allow enforcement agents to be more focused.[38] Evidence from other countries suggests that fortified enforcement can significantly decrease the number of counterfeit drugs in the market. In Nigeria, for example, Dora Akunyili's aggressive campaign to crack down on fake drugs resulted in a push to arrest landlords of apartments where fake drugs are stored, the conviction of more than fifty counterfeiters, and the shutting down of Onitsha Bridge Head Market, as discussed in chapter 3. As previously mentioned, WHO reported in 2002 that 70 percent of drugs in Nigeria were fake or substandard; by 2006, after Akunyili's successes, that figure had fallen to 16 percent.[39]

Policymakers should encourage self-regulation within the supply chain by endorsing reputable, independent regulatory organizations. Punitive measures are still only part of the solution to the problem of drug counterfeiting. Only increased monitoring activity by technically qualified laboratories, combined with concerted policing and consumer and supply-chain vigilance, will reduce criminal manufacturing and trafficking in fake drugs.[40]

Since the FDA and other government agencies cannot be omnipresent, they should encourage the credentialing work of other reputable, independent regulatory organizations to help consumers distinguish between online pharmacies from which it is safe to buy and those that are unsafe, as the FDA is doing with some Canadian online pharmacies. Building widespread legitimacy for these organizations will leave market actors with no choice but to adopt their services.

At the Business Level

Pharmaceutical companies must alert both the public and law enforcement officials to the distribution of counterfeit versions of their own drugs when they discover them. By fostering an environment of openness, pharmaceutical companies will help ensure a safe drug supply and keep the trust of their customers.

When appropriate, pharmaceutical companies should bypass small wholesalers and deal either directly with distributors or with only one trusted wholesaler. Pfizer is one company that is doing this.[41] Care must be taken, however, to strike a balance between preserving drug safety and promoting consumer-friendly competition. Purchasing directly from almost all manufacturers will likely add costs to the system—what James C. McAllister, editor of *Pharmacy Times,* describes as a "definite step backwards in supply chain management."[42]

Pharmaceutical companies are also uniquely positioned to provide consultative assistance and the transfer of technology to improve supply chains in low-income nations. They should be prepared to do so for any country that unequivocally defends intellectual property rights. They can only make investments for training and other support in these countries, however, if they are able to tier their prices appropriately. Currently, companies are looking to withdraw investment from some locations because of lack of patent protection and opposition to tiered pricing.[43]

At the Individual Level

Ultimately, each consumer is responsible for the medicines he or she takes. Consumers should be educated to understand the consequences—for their own health, for the health of the community, and for future innovation in drug development—of purchasing drugs outside of the standard supply chain. Drug companies and public agencies should work together to educate the public, buttressing a last-resort defense against the spread of fakes and making it possible for individuals to take charge of this aspect of their health care.

The public and private sectors should work together to educate individuals. Pharmacists and consumers at the point of sale are an important front line of defense in the drug supply chain. Today, many individuals are ignorant of the vast proliferation of, and danger posed by, counterfeit drugs; a 2006 poll commissioned by the National Consumers League found that 37 percent of consumers in the United States were completely unaware of the wholesale distribution system and, by extension, the possibility that counterfeit drugs might be inserted into the U.S. pharmaceutical supply chain.[44] Awareness remains low in many developing countries as well. One survey conducted in Laos found that 62 percent of customers believed "all drugs were of good quality." In urban areas 8 percent of customers, and 96 percent of those in rural and remote areas, said they had never heard that drugs could contain lower amounts of active ingredients than were allowed.[45] Even when aware of potential counterfeits, consumers—especially those in lower-income groups—may be tempted to go for what appear to be harmless bargains. Commenting on the case of Marcia Bergeron, the first person whose death was officially linked to counterfeit pharmaceuticals purchased online, Marnie Mitchell of the British Columbia Pharmacy Association recommended that the Canadian government launch a public awareness campaign to warn people of the potential dangers.[46]

Several steps can be taken to inform actors at the point of sale. For Internet consumers, a validation system can be created, in which pharmacies approved by the FDA, USP, or another reputable body carry a unique tracked logo. Any website posting the logo without permission could be spotted in a second and shut down by legal authorities. Such a system would build on the voluntary national Verified Internet Pharmacy Practice Sites (VIPPS) list maintained by the NABP in the United States and the mandatory Internet Pharmacy Logo system maintained by the Royal Pharmaceutical Society of Great Britain (RPSGB). In the NABP system, by paying a nominal fee and demonstrating compliance with its state's regulatory standards as well as NABP's, a pharmacy can display a linked VIPPS symbol on its website. To date, fifteen pharmacies have successfully applied for and implemented the VIPPS logo on their sites. The FDA might consider creating incentives for membership in VIPPS, especially for small, independent pharmacies.[47] The RPSGB system, which is mandatory for all pharmacies, features a logo with the online pharmacy's unique RPSGB membership number posted on the pharmacy's site. The logo links back to the RPSGB registration page, allowing customers to verify its veracity.[48]

Pharmacists in developed countries can be equipped with the latest anticounterfeiting and authentication technologies, and through partnerships with pharmacists in the developing world, they can facilitate the transfer of this technology. In some places, text messages might be used to alert consumers of compromised products. Security inks, invisible digital graphics and dots, surface fingerprinting, and infrared invisible codes might also be used, depending on cost-effectiveness.[49]

National governments and international organizations can promote "whistleblowing" by offering incentives to pharmacists, traders, and even consumers to report information leading to arrests or prosecutions of counterfeiters. A whistleblower hotline might be established, hosted by a national government or a non-governmental interested party such as U.S. Pharmacopeia.

Conclusion

While data are limited, there is little doubt that counterfeit drugs are an increasing problem globally, with hundreds of thousands of people dying annually as a result. Fakes are made and used primarily in locations where limited regulations allow illicit businesses to flourish, notably India, China, and Russia. With slightly better policing and product labeling in the West, counterfeiting can be held at bay, limited on the whole to parallel trading in Europe and to internet sales in the United States, where drugs come mainly from Asia. Western governments, NGOs, pharmaceutical companies, and international agencies can provide expertise on making top-down changes to legal systems and policing, as well as media-driven education to all but the poorest consumers. Western players can also help poor countries by improving bottom-up measurement of the counterfeiting problem, and by training and equipping distributors to identify fake drugs.

Even against a background of poverty and corruption, determined action by regulatory agencies can reduce drug counterfeiting, as evidenced by the progress that has been made in Nigeria; but the political will of sovereign nations must be exerted to make such change possible. Trading partners have significant leverage and can continue to press for reform on counterfeit manufacture and trade, particularly in China and India. While high-profile executions and new laws will not drastically reduce drug counterfeiting, increased policing, improvements to customs, and the education of traders can accomplish much. Some countries, especially in the African continent, will probably continue to need financial assistance from the international community. Yet even without such funds, resource-constrained countries can make changes at the margin. By chipping away at the small things and building a healthy policy framework, counterfeits can be fought—one pill at a time.

Notes

Introduction

1. Tim Phillips, *Knockoff: The Deadly Trade in Counterfeit Goods* (London: Kogan Page, 2005), 7.

2. Old Bailey Proceedings Online, "Thomas Rogers, Anne Rogers, Offences against the King: Coining, Miscellaneous: Perverting Justice, 15th October, 1690," *Proceedings of the Old Bailey*, reference no. t16901015–36, www.hrionline.ac.uk/luceneweb/bailey/highlight.jsp?ref=t16901015-36 (accessed March 17, 2008).

3. Margaret Zierdt, "Path Breakers," National Women's History Project (July 2007), http://www.nwhp.org/resourcecenter/pathbreakers.php (accessed January 16, 2008).

4. U.S. Secret Service, Counterfeit Division, "History of Counterfeiting," www.treas.gov/usss/counterfeit.shtml (accessed March 17, 2008).

5. James N. Green and Peter Stallybrass, "Job Printing," *Benjamin Franklin: Writer and Printer*, Library Company of Philadelphia, 2006, www.librarycompany.org/BFWriter/job.htm (accessed March 17, 2008).

6. World Health Organization, "Counterfeit Drugs: Guidelines for the Development of Measures to Combat Counterfeit Drugs," Document Prepared by the Department of Essential Drugs and Other Medicines, WHO, Geneva, Switzerland, 1999, http://whqlibdoc.who.int/hq/1999/WHO_EDM_QSM_99.1.pdf (accessed March 20, 2008).

7. As early as the first century AD, Greek physician Dioscorides identified the danger of counterfeit medicines. Adrian Johns, "When authorship met authenticity," *Nature* 451 (February 27, 2008), 1058–59.

8. U.S. Pharmacopeia is the official standard-setting authority for all prescription and over-the-counter medicines, dietary supplements, and other health-care products manufactured and sold in the United States. USP sets standards for the quality of these products that are recognized and used in more than 130 countries and works with health-care providers to help them achieve the standards. The independent, science-based public health organization is funded through revenues from the sale of products and services that help

ensure good pharmaceutical care, and its contributions to public health are enhanced by the participation and oversight of volunteers representing the pharmaceutical industry, health-care professions, academia, government, insurers, and consumer organizations. See U.S. Pharmacopeia, "USP History," 2007, www.usp.org/aboutUSP/history.html (accessed March 17, 2008). For the definition of "formulary," see Coalition Working Group, *Principles of a Sound Drug Formulary System*, October 2000, www.usp.org/pdf/EN/patient Safety/pSafetySndFormPrinc.pdf (March 17, 2008).

9. John Parry Griffin and John O'Grady, *The Textbook of Pharmaceutical Medicine* (London: British Medical Journal Publishing Group, 2002), 568.

10. Jake Hooker, "Chinese Company Linked to Deaths Wasn't Licensed," *New York Times*, May 9, 2007, http://www.nytimes.com/2007/05/09/world/asia/09china.html (accessed March 27, 2008).

11. World Health Organization, "Counterfeit Medicines," Fact Sheet 275, November 14, 2006, www.who.int/mediacentre/factsheets/fs275/en/index.html (accessed March 17, 2008).

12. Ibid.

13. World Health Organization, "General Information on Counterfeit Medicines," http://www.who.int/medicines/services/counterfeit/overview/en (accessed January 11, 2008).

14. World Health Organization, *Effective Drug Regulation: A Multicountry Study* (Geneva: World Health Organization, 2002), www.who.int/medicine docs/index.fcgi?sid=fFYQnGxO9ee80ca700000000474dcd26&a=d&c=me dicinedocs&d=Js2300e.6#Js2300e.6 (accessed March 19, 2008).

15. Good manufacturing practice (GMP) guidelines articulate baseline standards for all aspects of pharmaceutical production, including starting materials, premises and equipment, and staff training and hygiene. Under WHO's definition, GMP also includes documented proof that correct procedures are consistently followed at each step in the manufacturing process. Some countries, including the United States, have formulated their own GMP requirements based on WHO requirements. See World Health Organization, "GMP Questions and Answers," www.who.int/medicines/areas/quality_safety/quality_assurance/gmp/en (accessed March 17, 2008).

16. E. C. Consten, J. T. van der Meer, F. de Wolf, H. A. Heij, P. C. Henny, and J. J. van Lanschot, "Risk of Iatrogenic Human Immunodeficiency Virus Infection through Transfusion of Blood Tested by Inappropriately Stored or Expired Rapid Antibody Assays in a Zambian Hospital," *Transfusion* 37:9 (1997), 930–34, doi:10.1046/j.1537-2995.1997.37997454020.x (accessed January 11, 2008). The assays had a sensitivity and specificity between 11 and 18 percent below their manufactured standard.

17. Roger Bate and Kathryn Boateng, "Bad Medicine in the Market," *AEI Health Policy Outlook* 8 (2007), www.aei.org/publication26368/ (accessed March 17, 2008).

18. In these countries (and others), many producers obtain licenses for export only, meaning that the drugs they produce may not be subject to even weak domestic regulation.

19. Technical Committee on the Pharmaceutical Manufacturing Plan for Africa, "First Meeting of the Technical Committee on the Pharmaceutical Manufacturing Plan for Africa," October 24–26, 2007, Addis Ababa, Ethiopia, www.africa-union.org/root/au/Conferences/2007/october/sa/Pharmaceutical/DOCS/REPORT.doc (accessed 20 December 2007).

20. Roger Bate, "Thai-ing Pharma Down," *Wall Street Journal Asia*, February 9, 2007, available at http://www.aei.org/publications/pubID.25585/ pub_detail.asp (accessed March 27, 2008).

Chapter 1: Counterfeiting Today

1. Philip Alden, "Counterfeit Drug Problems, Deaths Kept Quiet by FDA," *San Mateo Daily Journal*, July 19, 2007, http://www.smdailyjournal.com/article_preview.php?id=76561&reddate=06/19/2007 (accessed March 27, 2008).

2. Ronald W. Buzzeo, "Counterfeit Pharmaceuticals and the Public Health," *Wall Street Journal*, October 4, 2005.

3. European Union-EUROPA, "European Commission Seeks Mandate to Negotiate Major New International Anti-Counterfeiting Pact," Press Release IP/07/1573, October 23, 2007, http://europa.eu/rapid/pressReleases Action.do?reference=IP/07/1573 (accessed January 14, 2008).

4. With a market worth more than $12 billion a year, Lipitor is a tempting target for fakers. Alex Berenson, "Lipitor or Generic? Billion-Dollar Battle Looms," *New York Times*, October 15, 2005, http://www.nytimes.com/2005/10/15/business/15statin.html (accessed March 17, 2008). High-value pharmaceuticals may be especially susceptible to "uplabeling," a counterfeiting technique in which low-dosage pills of a given drug are packaged—and passed off—as higher-dosage pills. Cancer medications such as Procrit have been targeted for uplabeling in recent years. See Katherine Eban, *Dangerous Doses: How Counterfeiters are Contaminating America's Drug Supply* (San Diego: Harcourt, 2005). Also see Nancy Shute, "Are Your Drugs Safe? Shoddy and Fraudulent Pharmacy Products Pose a Growing Threat," October 5, 2007, http://health.usnews.com/articles/health/2007/10/05/are-your-drugs-safe.html?PageNr=3 (accessed January 11, 2008).

5. Ten million American diabetes patients use LifeScan's OneTouch test strips to test their blood sugar levels. When complaints were made to the company in 2006 that the test strips were faulty, an investigation identified counterfeits from China, approximately one million of which had been sent to at least thirty-five states in the United States, as well as Canada, Greece, India, Pakistan, the Philippines, Saudi Arabia, and Turkey. Allan Dodds Frank and Lisa Rapaport, "Johnson & Johnson Tracks Down Maker of Phony Diabetes Test," *Bloomberg News*, August 16, 2007, http://www.bloomberg.com/apps/news?pid=20601103&sid=a5XA7.yplw9 k&refer=news (accessed March 27, 2008).

6. Randall Lutter (testimony on pharmaceutical supply chain security, Subcommittee on Criminal Justice, Drug Policy and Human Resources, U.S. House of Representatives, July 11,   2006), http://www.hhs.gov/asl/testify/t060711.html (accessed March 20, 2008).

7. BBC News, "Fake Obesity Drugs Are Discovered," September 2, 2004, http://news.bbc.co.uk/2/hi/health/3622400.stm (accessed March 27, 2008).

8. Anna Lewcock, "MHRA Launches New Action Plan to Combat UK Counterfeit Hub," in-Pharma, November 26, 2007, www.drugresearcher.com/news/ng.asp?n=81623-mhra-counterfeit-drug-fakes-who (accessed March 17, 2008).

9. BBC News, "Gang Guilty of Fake Viagra Scam," September 17, 2007, http://news.bbc.co.uk/2/hi/uk_news/6999160.stm (accessed March 27, 2008).

10. U.S. Government Accountability Office, "Report to the Chairman, Permanent Subcommittee on Investigations, Committee on Governmental Affairs, U.S. Senate: Internet Pharmacies: Some Pose Safety Risks for Consumers" (June 2004), http://www.gao.gov/new.items/d04820.pdf (accessed January 17, 2008).

11. The website was www.chinamerck.com. Personal communication with the author, August 29, 2007.

12. U.S. Food and Drug Administration, "FDA Warns Consumers about Counterfeit Drugs from Multiple Internet Sellers," news release, May 1, 2007, www.fda.gov/bbs/topics/NEWS/2007/NEW01623.html (accessed March 17, 2008).

13. Ibid.

14. U.S. Food and Drug Administration, "Authentic and Counterfeit Contraceptive Patches," www.fda.gov/bbs/topics/news/photos/contraceptive/counterfeit.html (accessed March 17, 2008).

15. Amanda Spake, "Fake Drugs, Real Worries," *U.S. News & World Report*, September 12, 2004, http://health.usnews.com/usnews/health/articles/040920/20internet.htm (accessed March 17, 2008).

16. Ibid.

17. U.S. Food and Drug Administration, "FDA Warns Consumers Not to Buy or Use Prescription Drugs from Various Canadian Websites that Apparently Sell Counterfeit Products," news release, August 20, 2006, http://www.fda.gov/bbs/topics/NEWS/2006/NEW01441.html (accessed March 17, 2008).

18. A counterfeit drug bust in Dubai in September 2007 revealed a complex supply chain of fake drugs that ran from China through Hong Kong, the United Arab Emirates, Britain, and the Bahamas, ultimately ending up at an Internet pharmacy advertised as Canadian. Walt Bogdanich, "Counterfeit Drugs' Path Eased by Free Trade Zones," *New York Times*, December 17, 2007, http://www.nytimes.com/2007/12/17/world/middleeast/17freezone.html (accessed March 27, 2008).

19. Randall W. Lutter (acting deputy commissioner for policy, Food and Drug Administration), "Policy Implications of Importing Drugs into the United States," (testimony, Subcommittee on Interstate Commerce, Trade, and Tourism Committee on Commerce, Science, and Transportation, U.S. Senate, March 7, 2007), http://commerce.senate.gov/public/index.cfm?FuseAction=Hearings.Testimony&Hearing_ID=1829&Witness_ID=6533 (accessed January 14, 2008).

20. U.S. Food and Drug Administration, "FDA Warns Consumers Not to Buy or Use Prescription Drugs from Various Canadian Websites."

21. Ibid.

22. *Pharma Marketletter*, "U.S. Counterfeit Drug Scam Used Internet Spam," October 3, 2006.

23. *Medical News Today*, "International Internet Drug Ring Shattered," April 24, 2005.

24. BBC News, "Gang Guilty of Fake Viagra Scam."

25. The MHRA noted changes in the types of medicines being faked, as well as an overall doubling of cases from 2001 through 2006. Lyndsay Moss, "Counterfeit Drug Cases Double as Gangs Target NHS Supply Chain," *Scotsman*, January 3, 2007.

26. Spake, "Fake Drugs, Real Worries."

27. *Sunday Times* (London), "Factory for Fake Prescription Drugs," September 23, 2007, http://www.timesonline.co.uk/tol/news/uk/health/article2511583.ece (accessed March 27, 2008).

28. World Health Organization, "General Information on Counterfeit Medicines," www.who.int/medicines/services/counterfeit/overview/en/index.html (accessed March 17, 2008).

29. Julian Morris and Philip Stevens, *Counterfeit Medicines in Less Developed Countries: Problems and Solutions* (London: International Policy Network and

Campaign for Fighting Diseases, May 2006), http://www.fightingdiseases.org/pdf/IPN_Counterfeits.pdf (accessed March 17, 2008).

30. Wyatt Yankus, *Counterfeit Drugs: Coming to a Pharmacy Near You* (American Council on Science and Health, 2006): 1, available at www.acsh.org/publications/pubID.1379/pub_detail.asp (accessed March 20, 2008).

31. Sania Nishtar, "Pharmaceuticals—Strategic Considerations in Health Reforms in Pakistan," *Journal of the Pakistan Medical Association* 56, no.12, supp. 4 (December 2006): 100–11.

32. Paul N. Newton, Nicholas J. White, Jan A. Rozendaal, and Michael D. Green, "Murder by Fake Drugs: Time for International Action," *British Medical Journal* 324 (April 6, 2002): 800–801.

33. Krystn Alter Hall, Paul N. Newton, Michael D. Green, Marleen De Veij, Peter Vandenabeele, David Pizzanelli, Mayfong Mayxay, Arjen Dondorp, and Facundo M. Fernandez, "Characterization of Counterfeit Artesunate Antimalarial Tablets from Southeast Asia," *American Journal of Tropical Medicine and Hygiene* 75, no. 5 (2006): 804–11.

34. Ibid.

35. Chloroquine remains one of the most widely used first-line antimalarials, even though the parasite has developed resistance to the drug in many areas of Africa due to widespread misuse. Nancy Blum, "Quality Control Approaches for Essential Medicines," World Bank conference, Washington, D.C., March 10, 2005, http://siteresources.worldbank.org/INTAFRREGTOP HIVAIDS/Resources/gibd.htm (accessed March 17, 2008). See also Charles Maponga and Clive Ondari, *The Quality of Antimalarials: A Study in Selected African Countries*, World Health Organization, 2003, http://whqlibdoc.who.int/hq/2003/WHO_EDM_PAR_2003.4.pdf (accessed March 17, 2008).

36. Roger Bate, "Fake!" *American*, September/October 2007, http://american.com/archive/2007/september-october-magazine-contents/counterfeits-kill (accessed March 17, 2008).

37. Reuters, "Government Inaction Spurs Consumption of Counterfeit Drugs," February 20, 2008, http://www.alertnet.org/thenews/newsdesk/IRIN/63414f02b64fb2d5616a935dc9b3145c.htm (accessed March 27, 2008).

38. Roger Bate and Kathryn Boateng, "Medicinal Malpractice," *AEI Health Policy Outlook* 10 (December 2006), www.aei.org/publication25276 (accessed March 17, 2008).

39. Voice of America, "Counterfeit Drug Sales in Africa Strong, Threaten Public Health," October 22, 2007.

40. P. S. Sow, T. S. N. Gueye, E. Sy, L. Toure, C. Ba, and M. Badiane, "Drugs in the Parallel Market for the Treatment of Urethral Discharge in Dakar: Epidemiological Investigation Physiochemical Tests," *International Journal of Infectious Diseases* 6, no. 2 (2002): 108–12.

41. Maria Christina Gaudiano, Anna Di Maggio, Emilia Cocchieri, Eleonora Antoniella, Paola Bertocchi, Stefano Alimonti, and Luisa Valvo, "Medicines Informal Market in Congo, Burundi and Angola: Counterfeit and Sub-Standard Antimalarials," *Malaria Journal* 6, no. 22 (February 22, 2007), www.malariajournal.com/content/6/1/22 (accessed March 17, 2008).

42. Joyce Primo-Carpenter and Milissa McGinnis, "Matrix of Drug Quality Reports in USAID-Assisted Countries" (U.S. Pharmacopeia, October 15, 2007), www.usp.org/pdf/EN/dqi/ghcDrugQualityMatrix (accessed March 17, 2008). Substandard drugs may pose as great a problem for Africans as fakes—and certainly greater problems for populations as a whole as resistance builds—but the evidence has yet to be fully collected and analyzed.

43. World Health Organization, International Medical Products Anti-Counterfeiting Taskforce (IMPACT), "Counterfeit Medicines: An Update On Estimates," November 15, 2006, www.who.int/medicines/services/counterfeit/impact/TheNewEstimatesCounterfeit.pdf (accessed March 17, 2008).

44. Ibid.

45. Acho Orabuchi, "Dangers of Drug Counterfeiting," *Leadership* (Abuja, Nigeria), October 25, 2007, http://allafrica.com/stories/200710250091.html (accessed March 27, 2008).

46. The author is aware that these "similares" stores are increasingly seen in Argentina, Peru, and Mexico, and perhaps elsewhere. No comprehensive study of drug quality has been undertaken of them.

47. Matías Loewy, "Deadly Imitations," *Perspectives in Health* 11, no. 1 (2007), www.paho.org/English/DD/PIN/Number23_article3.htm (accessed March 17, 2008).

48. Ibid.

49. Tom Parfitt, "Russia Cracks Down on Counterfeit Drugs," *Lancet* 368, no. 9546 (2006):1481–82.

50. Ibid.

51. The Coalition for Intellectual Property Rights is a public-private partnership dedicated to advancing intellectual property rights protection, enforcement, and reform in the Commonwealth of Independent States and the Baltic states. Andrew E. Kramer, "Russia's New Specialty: Fake Pharmaceuticals: Copies Range from Crude to Exquisite," *International Herald Tribune*, September 5, 2006, http://www.iht.com/articles/2006/09/05/business/drug.php (accessed March 17, 2008).

52. Ibid.

53. Parfitt, "Russia Cracks Down."

54. Ibid.

55. Ibid.

56. Ibid.

57. Personal communication with several intellectual property investigators, including Vijay Karan (former chief of police, New Delhi, India), January 16 and 17, 2008.

58. European Commission Taxation and Customs Union, "Summary of Community Customs Activities on Counterfeit and Piracy," 2006, http://ec.europa.eu/taxation_customs/resources/documents/customs/customs_controls/counterfeit_piracy/statistics/counterf_comm_2006_en.pdf (accessed March 28, 2008).

59. Marc Kaufman, "FDA Scrutiny Scant in India, China as Drugs Pour into U.S.," *Washington Post*, June 17, 2007, A1, http://www.washingtonpost.com/wp-dyn/content/article/2007/06/16/AR2007061601295. html (accessed March 27, 2008).

60. As an opinion piece in the *Wall Street Journal* notes, penetration of counterfeit products such as adulterated Chinese toothpaste are exceedingly rare in the United States precisely because "companies have every incentive to police themselves." Think of Mattel and its "toy import nightmare," for example. *Wall Street Journal*, "The Real FDA Scandal," February 6, 2008, A18.

61. IMPACT, which will be discussed in greater detail in chapter 3, is a voluntary WHO program which all 193 member states have joined. It aims to eliminate the production, trading, and selling of fake medicines.

62. Personal communication with Karan; Suresh Sati, a consultant who investigates abuses of intellectual property rights on behalf of private companies; and Dr. Uday Shankar (pharmacist at the Indian Government Hospital), January 16 and 17, 2008.

63. Government of India, Ministry of Health, "A Report of the Expert Committee on 'A Comprehensive Examination of Drug Regulatory Issues, Including the Problem of Spurious Drugs,'" November 2003, http://cdsco.nic.in/html/Final%20Report%20mashelkar.pdf (accessed February 29, 2008). Based on samples tested by the state authorities between 1995 and 2003, the extent of substandard drugs varied from 8.19 to 10.64 percent. The extent of spurious drugs varied between 0.24 and 0.47 percent. Industry and police sources say this number is too low, however, and place the number of spurious drugs between 10 and 20 percent.

64. World Health Organization, "Counterfeit Medicines"; and World Health Organization, IMPACT, "Counterfeit Medicines: An Update On

Estimates." Sources for both reports were industry bodies, which must be presumed to know their own markets. While they have an incentive to wax overly rosy about the quality of their markets, they do point to the scale of the problem. Note, however, that the period over which illegal drugs in India has grown is not given, rendering the information of limited value. The Chinese data are limited to estimates of drugs sold in pharmacies; informal markets remain murky. Moreover, these figures, which point to the scale of the problem, are not likely to represent its true scope because they only address domestic counterfeit penetration. Most illegal drugs in Nigeria, for example, are imported from China and India.

65. Hall et al., "Characterization of Counterfeit Artesunate Antimalarial Tablets from Southeast Asia."

Chapter 2: How and Why Does Counterfeiting Occur?

1. Rajendrani Mukhopadhyay, "The Hunt for Counterfeit Medicine," *Analytical Chemistry* 79, no. 7 (2007): 2623–37. Researchers have recently discovered that counterfeiters now include tiny amounts of the active ingredient in response to the introduction of basic colorimetric testing done to check for counterfeits.

2. Roger Bate, "Thailand and the Drug Patent Wars," *AEI Health Policy Outlook* 5 (April 2007), www.aei.org/publication25890 (accessed March 17, 2008).

3. Anupama Sukhlecha, "Counterfeit and Substandard Quality of Drugs: The Need for an Effective and Stringent Regulatory Control in India and Other Developing Countries," letter, *Indian Journal of Pharmacology* 39, no. 4 (August 2007): 206–7.

4. Maureen Lewis, "Governance and Corruption in Public Health Care Systems," Working Paper 78, Center for Global Development, Washington, D.C., January 2006, www.cgdev.org/files/5967_file_WP_78.pdf (accessed March 17, 2008).

5. Ibid.

6. Monica Das Gupta, Varun Gauri, and Stuti Khemani, "Decentralized Delivery of Primary Health Services in Nigeria: Survey Evidence from the States of Lagos and Kogi" (World Bank, 2004).

7. Maureen Lewis, "Governance and Corruption in Public Health Care Systems."

8. Barbara McPake, Delius Asiimwe, Francis Mwesigye, Mathias Ofumbib, Lisbeth Ortenbladd, Pieter Stree, and Asaph Turinde, "Informal Economic Activities of Public Health Workers in Uganda: Implications for

Quality and Accessibility of Care," *Social Science and Medicine* 49 (1999): 849–65.

9. Rafael Di Tella and William D. Savedoff, eds., *Diagnosis Corruption: Fraud in Latin America's Public Hospitals* (Washington, D.C.: Inter-American Development Bank, 2001), 15.

10. G8 Group, "Fight Against Infectious Diseases" (summit statement, St. Petersburg, Russia, July 16, 2006), http://en.g8russia.ru/docs/10.html (accessed March 17, 2008).

11. Katherine Eban, *Dangerous Doses: How Counterfeiters are Contaminating America's Drug Supply* (San Diego: Harcourt, 2005), 89–92.

12. Ibid.

13. George E. Jordan, "Fake Medicine, Real Problem," *Star-Ledger*, October 22, 2007.

14. Eban, *Dangerous Doses*. Pharmaceutical company insiders have expressed similar sentiments in personal communication with the author.

15. Ibid.

16. Gilbert M. Gaul and Mary Pat Flaherty, "U.S. Prescription Drug System Under Attack," *Washington Post*, October 19, 2003, A1, http://www.washingtonpost.com/ac2/wp-dyn/A44908-2003Oct18 (accessed March 27, 2008).

17. Ibid.

18. Eban, *Dangerous Doses*, 92.

19. Ibid. This was confirmed by an FDA official, who asked not to be quoted by name: "Frankly, there are sometimes bigger fish to fry." Personal communication with the author, September 12, 2007.

20. Eban, *Dangerous Doses*.

21. Ibid., 20.

22. Anonymous FDA official, September 12, 2007.

23. U.S. Government Accountability Office, *Drug Safety: Preliminary Findings Suggest Weaknesses in FDA's Program for Inspecting Foreign Drug Manufacturers* (congressional testimony, Subcommittee on Oversight and Investigations, Committee on Energy and Commerce, U.S. House of Representatives, November 1, 2007), www.gao.gov/new.items/d08224t.pdf (accessed March 17, 2008); and *MQN Weekly Bulletin*, "Lawmakers Debate Import Safety, How to Stop Counterfeit Drugs," October 5, 2007, http://www.fdanews.com/newsletter/article?articleId=99407&issueId=10820 (accessed March 17, 2008).

24. National Consumers League, "Counterfeit Drugs Survey," July 20, 2004, www.nclnet.org/pressroom/fakedrugsreport.htm (accessed March 17, 2008).

25. Roger Bate and Kathryn Boateng, "Drug Pricing and Its Discontents," *AEI Health Policy Outlook* 9 (August 2007), www.aei.org/publication26622 (accessed March 17, 2008).

26. *Pharma Marketletter*, "Fake Parallel Trade Drugs Hit UK, Product Recalls Issued by the MHRA," May 29, 2007.

27. *Pharma Marketletter*, "Warning about Continued Dangers of Counterfeit Prescription Drugs from NABP," January 12, 2007.

28. BBC News, "Fake Medicines 'A Growing Menace,'" November 22, 2006, http://news.bbc.co.uk/2/hi/health/6166324.stm (accessed March 27, 2008).

29. *Les Echos* (France), "Increase in Counterfeit Goods Seized in France," March 22, 2005.

30. "Counterfeit Medicines Pass through Finland to World Markets," *Helsingin Sanomat*, June 14, 2007, http://www.hs.fi/english/article/Counterfeit+medicines+pass+through+Finland+to+world+markets/1135228018377 (accessed March 21, 2008).

31. Estimate as of July 2007. Central Intelligence Agency, *World Fact Book*, "Finland," December 6, 2007, https://www.cia.gov/library/publications/the-world-factbook/geos/fi.html (accessed March 20, 2008).

32. *Helsingin Sanomat*, "Counterfeit Medicines Pass Through Finland to World Markets."

33. Luc De Wulf and Jose B. Sokol, eds., *Customs Modernization Handbook* (Washington, D.C.: World Bank, 2005).

34. Roger Bate, Richard Tren, Lorraine Mooney, and Kathryn Boateng, "Tariffs, Corruption and Other Impediments to Medicinal Access in Developing Countries: Field Evidence," Working Paper 130, American Enterprise Institute, August 4, 2006, www.aei.org/publication24749 (accessed March 17, 2008).

35. Ibid.

36. Ibid.

37. Karina Rollins, ed., *The Index of Global Philanthropy* 2006 (Washington, D.C.: Hudson Institute, 2006).

38. Gilbert Cruz, "Filling Holes in the Food Supply," *Time*, July 18, 2007, http://www.time.com/time/health/article/0,8599,1644705,00.html (accessed March 27, 2008). Representative Jay Inslee (D-Wash.) commented on the growing concern in the United States over Chinese food exports: "Who Needs al Qaeda When You Have Got E. Coli?" While the content of Inslee's response may be extreme, its tone is not atypical. Indeed, there have been many warnings about the dangers of Chinese exports, including some that exaggerated the threat posed to consumers. In May 2007, the editor of *The Consumerist*, a

leading consumer-advocacy blog, warned consumers of a "Chinese Poison Train . . . lurking on a container ship headed our way." (http://consumerist.com/consumer/diethylene-glycol/chinese-poison-train-defeats-fda-the-prequel-269627.php, accessed March 20, 2008). In a similar fashion, *WorldNetDaily* alluded to insidious intent from the East Asian giant, entitling one of its articles with the provocative question, "Is China Trying to Poison Americans and Their Pets?" http://www.wnd.com/news/article.asp?ARTICLE_ID=55892 (accessed March 17, 2008). See also Jeff Yang, "A Taste of Racism in the Chinese Food Scare," *Washington Post*, July 15, 2007, B2.

39. Wyatt Yankus, *Counterfeit Drugs: Coming to a Pharmacy Near You* (American Council on Science and Health, 2006), available at www.acsh.org/publications/pubID.1379/pub_detail.asp, page 2 (accessed March 21, 2008).

40. Ibid.

41. Victoria Colliver, "Bogus Drugs a Growing Threat," *San Francisco Chronicle*, August 3, 2003, A1, http://www.sfgate.com/cgi-bin/article.cgi?file=/c/a/2003/08/03/FAKEDRUGS.TMP&type=health (accessed March 27, 2008).

42. Kerry Capell, Suzanne Timmons, Jonathan Wheatley, and Heidi Dawley, "What's In That Pill?" *BusinessWeek*, June 18, 2001, http://www.businessweek.com/magazine/content/01_25/b3737076.htm (accessed March 27, 2008).

43. Ibid.

44. Randy Barnett, "Fighting Crime without Punishment," in *The Structure of Liberty: Justice and the Rule of Law* (Oxford: Oxford University Press, 2004), chapter 11.

45. Barnett, "Fighting Crime Without Punishment."

46. Randy Barnett, personal communication with author, October 2004. See also ibid.

47. Robert Pear, "U.S. Health Chief, Stepping Down, Issues Warning," *New York Times*, December 4, 2004, http://www.nytimes.com/2004/12/04/politics/04health.html (accessed March 27, 2008).

48. Bryan A. Liang, "Safety of Drug Supply: Tougher Laws Needed to Stem Counterfeit Drug Rings," *Daily Transcript* (San Diego), May 4, 2006, www.sddt.com/News/article.cfm?SourceCode=20060503crd (accessed June 7, 2007).

49. U.S. Chamber of Commerce, National Chamber Foundation, "Anti-Counterfeiting and Piracy Update," May 2006, http://www.uschamber.com/NR/rdonlyres/evv2revsokapuvbwv7felwdebvub477qfaixdkj62grs452brdiupukcq27pvczholyq3ykzsdtdzzhcyuvu35asv7h/MicrosoftWordOutrageoftheMonthFundingTerrorismMay2006.pdf (accessed January 28, 2008).

50. Liza Gibson, "Drug Regulators Study Global Treaty to Tackle Counterfeit Drugs," *British Medical Journal* 328:7438 (February 28, 2004):

486, also available at http://www.bmj.com/cgi/content/full/328/7438/486-c (accessed January 28, 2008).

51. Armina Ligaya, "Counterfeit Drugs Caused Woman's Death, Coroner Concludes," *Globe and Mail*, July 6, 2007, http://www.buysafedrugs.info/Reports/Counterfeit_Drugs_Caused_Womans_Death.html (accessed March 27, 2008).

52. Roger Bate, "On the Trail of a Cure: Reality and Rhetoric on Treating Malaria," *AEI Health Policy Outlook* 4 (March 2007), www.aei.org/publication 25834 (accessed March 17, 2008).

Chapter 3: Stopping the Fakers

1. World Health Organization, *Declaration of Rome* (WHO International Conference on Combating Counterfeit Medicines, Rome, February 18, 2006), http://www.who.int/medicines/services/counterfeit/RomeDeclaration.pdf (accessed March 17, 2008).

2. IMPACT includes the following organizations: Interpol, the Organisation for Economic Co-operation and Development, the World Customs Organization, the World Intellectual Property Organization, the World Trade Organization, the International Federation of Pharmaceutical and Manufacturers' Associations, the International Generic Pharmaceuticals Alliance, the World Self-Medication Industry, the Asociación Latino-americana de Industrias Farmacéuticas, the World Bank, the European Commission, the Council of Europe, the Commonwealth Secretariat, the Association of Southeast Asian Nations Secretariat, the International Federation of Pharmaceutical Wholesalers, the European Association of Pharmaceutical Full-line Wholesalers, the International Pharmaceutical Federation, the International Council of Nurses, the World Medical Association, and Pharmaciens Sans Frontières (Pharmacists Without Borders). World Health Organization, International Medical Products Anti-Counterfeiting Taskforce (IMPACT), "Frequently Asked Questions," http://www.who.int/impact/impact_q-a/en/index.html (accessed March 17, 2008).

3. Agence France-Presse, "Interpol to Fight Sale of Fake Medicines in Africa," November 11, 2007, http://www.aegis.com/NEWS/AFP/2007/AF071114.html (accessed March 27, 2008).

4. World Health Organization, *Declaration of Rome*.

5. World Health Organization, "Report of the Commission on Intellectual Property Rights, Innovation, and Public Health," 2006, http://www.who.int/intellectualproperty/documents/thereport/ENPublicHealthReport.pdf (accessed March 20, 2008), 15.

6. Paul D'Eramo, "Japan's Pharmaceutical Affairs Law (PAL): Opportunities and Challenges," http://www.ispe.org/cs/root/regulatory_resources/regulatory_review_article_archives/february_2007_japans_pharmaceutical_affairs_law_pal_opportunities_and_challenges (accessed March 17, 2008).

7. Japan, Ministry of Health, Labour and Welfare, Pharmaceutical and Food Safety Bureau, Compliance and Narcotics Division, "Importing or Bringing Medication into Japan for Personal Use," April 1, 2004, http://www.mhlw.go.jp/english/topics/import/index.html (accessed February 8, 2008).

8. Japan, Ministry of Health, Labour and Welfare, Pharmaceuticals and Medical Safety Bureau, "The Pharmaceutical Affairs Law," http://www5.cao.go.jp/otodb/english/houseido/hou/lh_02070.html (accessed March 17, 2008).

9. D'Eramo, "Japan's Pharmaceutical Affairs Law."

10. U.S. International Trade Commission, *Medical Devices and Equipment: Competitive Conditions Affecting U.S. Trade in Japan and Other Principal Foreign Markets*, March 2007, http://hotdocs.usitc.gov/ docs/Pubs/332/Pub 3909.pdf (accessed February 8, 2008).

11. Ilisa B.G. Bernstein, "Impact of the PDMA on the Pharmaceutical Supply Chain," NACDS/HDMA RFID Adoption Summit, U.S. FDA, November 13, 2006, www.fda.gov/oc/initiatives/counterfeit/hdmanadcs 1113_files/textmostly/slide3.html (accessed March 17, 2008).

12. Amanda Spake, "Fake Drugs, Real Worries," *U.S. News & World Report*, September 12, 2004, http://health.usnews.com/usnews/health/articles/040920/20internet.htm (accessed March 17, 2008).

13. David Hess, "Rising Tide of Legitimate Drug Imports Threatens FDA's Ability to Ensure Safety," *Congress Daily AM*, June 5, 2007.

14. U.S. Food and Drug Administration, *Combating Counterfeit Drugs: A Report of the Food and Drug Administration Annual Update*, May 18, 2005, http://www.fda.gov/oc/initiatives/counterfeit/report02_04.html (March 17, 2008).

15. *Economic Times* (India), "U.S. wants FDA inspectors stationed in India," March 19, 2008, http://timesofindia.indiatimes.com/USA/US_wants_FDA_inspectors_stationed_in_India/articleshow/2880547.cms (accessed March 27, 2008).

16. Committee on Energy and Commerce, "Committee Panel to Hold Hearings on Heparin Failures," news release, U.S. House of Representatives, March 19, 2008, http://energycommerce.house.gov/Press_110/110nr187.shtml (accessed March 27, 2008).

17. See discussion of parallel trading on pages 31–33 in chapter 2, "How and Why Does Counterfeiting Occur?"

18. World Intellectual Property Organization, "Danish Experience on Anticounterfeiting Training and Awareness Raising Activities," www.wipo. int/edocs/mdocs/enforcement/en/wipo_ace_3/wipo_ace_3_www_61112.pdf (accessed March 17, 2008).

19. Partnership for Safe Medicines, "Counterfeit Drugs in Europe Fact Sheet," 2005, www.safemedicines.org/resources/europe.pdf (accessed March 17, 2008).

20. Between 1956 and 1962, thalidomide was prescribed and sold to pregnant women to combat morning sickness and help them sleep. Ten thousand children were born with severe malformity before the teratogenic properties of the drug were discovered.

21. Graham Satchwell, *A Sick Business: Counterfeit Medicines and Organized Crime* (London: Stockholm Network, 2004), 26–27.

22. World Health Organization, *Effective Drug Regulation: A Multi-country Study* (Geneva: World Health Organization, 2002), www.who.int/ medicinedocs/index.fcgi?sid=fFYQnGxO9ee80ca700000000474 dcd26&a=d&c=medicinedocs&d=Js2300e.6#Js2300e.6 (accessed March 19, 2008).

23. Roger Bate, "Thailand and the Drug Patent Wars," *AEI Health Policy Outlook* 5 (April 2007), www.aei.org/publication25890 (accessed March 17, 2008).

24. For discussion of data collection difficulties, particularly a lack of reliable statistics, see pages 19–20 in chapter 1, "Counterfeiting Today."

25. Joyce Primo-Carpenter and Milissa McGinnis, "Matrix of Drug Quality Reports in USAID-Assisted Countries" U.S. Pharmacopeia, October 15, 2007, www.usp.org/pdf/EN/dqi/ghcDrugQualityMatrix (accessed March 17, 2008).

26. Wyatt Yankus, *Counterfeit Drugs: Coming to a Pharmacy Near You* (American Council on Science and Health, 2006), 3, complete study available at www.acsh.org/publications/pubID.1379/pub_detail.asp (accessed March 21, 2008).

27. See discussion in chapter 1, note 63.

28. Primo-Carpenter and McGinnis, "Matrix of Drug Quality Reports in USAID-Assisted Countries."

29. World Health Organization, IMPACT, "Counterfeit Medicines: An Update on Estimates," November 15, 2006, www.who.int/medicines/ services/counterfeit/impact/TheNewEstimatesCounterfeit.pdf.

30. Ibid.

31. Dora Akunyili, "IMPACT—A New Force in Global Anticounterfeiting" (presentation, Third Global Forum on Pharmaceutical Anti-Counterfeiting,

Prague, Czech Republic, March 15, 2007); Primo-Carpenter and McGinnis, "Matrix of Drug Quality Reports in USAID-Assisted Countries."

32. Nigeria officially blacklisted nineteen different Indian and Chinese companies from exporting drugs into the country because of their confirmed counterfeiting practices. Dora Akunyili, "Counterfeit and Substandard Drugs, Nigeria's Experience: Implications, Challenges, Actions and Recommendations" (presentation, World Bank, Washington, D.C., March 11, 2005), http://siteresources.worldbank.org/INTAFRREG-TOPHIVAIDS/Resources/717089-1113520923653/Dora_Akunyili-Good_Intentions-Bad_Drugs-MAR_10_05.doc (accessed March 17, 2008).

33. Dora Akunyili, "Tackling the Scourge of Counterfeit Drugs in Nigeria" (keynote speech, Twelfth Annual Convention and Scientific Assembly, Association of Nigerian Physicians in the Americas, New Brunswick, N.J., July 5–9, 2006), http://www.anpa.org/newsdetailsa.php?start1=5 (accessed March 21, 2008).

34. Akunyili, "Counterfeit and Substandard Drugs, Nigeria's Experience."

35. Akunyili, "Tackling the Scourge."

36. U.S. Pharmacopeia, "Ensuring the Quality of Medicines in Low-Income Countries: An Operational Guide, Draft for Field Testing," U.S. Agency for International Development (September 2005), 38, also available at http://www.usp.org/pdf/EN/dqi/ensuringQualityOperational Guide.pdf (accessed March 27, 2008).

37. Sauwakon Ratanawijitrasin and Eshetu Wondemagegnehu, "Effective Drug Regulation: A Multicountry Study" (World Health Organization, 2002), http://www.who.int/medicinedocs/collect/medicinedocs/pdf/s2300e/s2300e.pdf (accessed March 17, 2008).

38. Ibid., 25.

39. Ibid.

40. Barry Bearak, "Zimbabwe: Inflation Surges to Official 66,000%," New York Times, February 15, 2008, http://www.nytimes.com/2008/02/15/world/africa/15briefs-inflation.html?ex=1360731600&en=bd7578 947022d10f&ei=5088&partner=rssnyt&emc=rss (accessed March 27, 2008).

41. Financial Gazette (Harare), "Fake ARVs Flood Country," July 26, 2007, http://allafrica.com/stories/200707260858.html (accessed February 25, 2008).

42. Ratanawijitrasin and Wondemagegnehu, "Effective Drug Regulation."

43. Financial Gazette (Harare), "Fake ARVs Flood Country."

44. Dagi Kimani, "Illegally Imported, Fake Drugs Flood Kenya," East African, May 10, 2004, http://www.nationaudio.com/News/EastAfrican/current/Features/PartII100520043.html (accessed February 29, 2008).

45. Dauti Kahura, "Finding Remedy for Drugs Industry," *Standard* (Kenya), October 10, 2005, http://216.180.252.4/archives/index.php?mnu =details&id=30237&catid=176 (accessed February 29, 2008).

46. Ibid.

47. Euromonitor International, *OTC Healthcare in Kenya*, executive summary, August 2006, http://www.euromonitor.com/OTC_Healthcare_in_ Kenya#exec (accessed February 29, 2008).

48. Kui Kinyanjui, "Counterfeit Drugs Expose Consumers to an Escalation in Health Conditions," *Business Daily* (Kenya), February 15, 2008, http://www.bdafrica.com/index.php?option=com_content&task=view&id= 5901&Itemid=5822 (accessed March 3, 2008).

49. World Health Organization, International Medical Products Anti-Counterfeiting Taskforce (IMPACT), "Counterfeit Medicines: An Update on Estimates."

50. Kahura, "Finding Remedy for Drugs Industry," and Dauti Kahura, "Weak Medicine," *Standard* (Kenya), August 17, 2005, http://216.180.252.4/ archives/index.php?mnu=details&id=27417&catid=77 (accessed March 17, 2008).

51. Kahura, "Weak Medicine."

52. For more information about the work of PAHO, PANDRH, and the Pharmaceutical Forum of the Americas, see PAHO's resources in Pan American Health Organization, "Drug Safety," http://www.paho.org/ Project.asp?SEL=TP&LNG=ENG&ID=176 (accessed March 17, 2008).

53. Pan American Health Organization, "Pan American Network for Drug Regulatory Harmonization (Norms and Regulations)," http://www.paho.org/ english/ad/ths/ev/norms-pandrh.pdf (accessed March 17, 2008).

54. World Health Organization, "Medicines Regulation," in *The World Medicines Situation*, 2004, chapter 9, http://www.searo.who.int/LinkFiles/ Reports_World_Medicines_Situation.pdf (accessed March 17, 2008).

55. See DIGEMID website, http://www.digemid.minsa.gob.pe (accessed March 3, 2008).

56. World Health Organization, International Medical Products Anti-Counterfeiting Taskforce (IMPACT), "Counterfeit Medicines: An Update on Estimates."

57. Ratanawijitrasin and Wondemagegnehu, "Effective Drug Regulation," 42.

58. Dennis E. Baker, associate commissioner for regulatory affairs, FDA, "Testimony on Counterfeit Bulk Drugs," House Subcommittee on Oversight and Investigations, Committee on Commerce, June 8, 2000, http://www.hhs.gov/asl/testify/t000608a.html (accessed March 28, 2008).

59. *WIPO Magazine*, "Global Congress on Combating Counterfeiting and Piracy: The First Three Years," January 2007, http://www.wipo.int/wipo_magazine/en/2007/01/article_0002.html (accessed March 17, 2008).

60. Tom Parfitt, "Russia Cracks Down on Counterfeit Drugs," *Lancet* 368, no. 9546 (2006):1481–82.

61. Ibid.

62. Ibid.

63. Hepeng Jia, "Disgraced Drug Chief Sentenced to Death," *Chemistry World*, May 30, 2007, www.rsc.org/chemistryworld/News/2007/May/30050701.asp (accessed March 17, 2008).

64. Organisation for Economic Co-operation and Development, *The Economic Impact of Counterfeiting and Piracy Summary*, executive summary, June 4, 2007, www.oecd.org/dataoecd/11/38/38704571.pdf (accessed March 17, 2008). A 2007 econometric analysis by the OECD found that while counterfeiting and piracy had no effect on the volume of international trade, it did tend to alter the type of goods exported and imported. Economies with relatively high counterfeiting and piracy rates tended to export lower shares of products for which health and safety concerns were high.

65. Ibid.

66. Reuters, "China to Extend 'Arduous' Drug Industry Clean-Up," December 4, 2007, http://www.reuters.com/article/worldNews/idUSPEK37076320071203 (accessed March 27, 2008).

67. CBS News, "China: Drug Safety Drive Showing Results," December 4, 2007, http://www.cbsnews.com/stories/2007/12/03/health/main3568091.shtml (accessed March 27, 2008).

68. Audra Ang, "Chinese Arrest 774 in Product Crackdown Attempt to Calm Importers' Fears," *Washington Post*, October 30, 2007, D1, http://www.washingtonpost.com/wp-dyn/content/article/2007/10/29/AR2007102900963.html (accessed March 27, 2008).

69.U.S. Trade Representative, *2007 Special 301 Report*, 2007, www.ustr.gov/assets/Document_Library/Reports_Publications/2007/2007_Special_301_Review/asset_upload_file230_11122.pdf (March 17, 2008).

70. Xinhua, "China to Impose Stiff Penalty on Fake Drug Makers, Dealers," November 29, 2007.

71. David Blumenthal and William Hsiao, "Privatization and Its Discontents: The Evolving Chinese System," *New England Journal of Medicine* 353, no. 11 (September 15, 2005): 1165–70.

72. Nicholas Zamiska, "U.S. Opens the Door to Chinese Pills: Approval of AIDS Medicine for 2012 Seen as First Shot in Generic Fight with India,"

Wall Street Journal, October 9, 2007, http://online.wsj.com/public/article_print/SB119187230072652477.html (accessed March 27, 2008).

73. Some officials, like Valerio Reggi, the World Health Organization's coordinator for medicines regulatory support, have suggested that the size of the counterfeit and substandard drug market in many industrializing countries, including India, may be exaggerated. C. H. Unnikrishnan, "World Health Organization Says Willing to Help in Fake Drugs Study," *Mint* (India), August 27, 2007, http://www.livemint.com/2007/08/25002014/World-Health-Organization-says.html (accessed March 27, 2008).

74. According to a nationwide survey released by the World Health Organization's Regional Office for South East Asia in May 2007, counterfeit drugs accounted for approximately 3 percent of all drugs assessed. But problems in survey design, including focus on "retail outlets near railway station/bus stands" and a lack of sample anonymity (many sellers suspected the researchers posing as customers were from a drug regulatory agency, an NGO, or were students interested in studying the quality of medicines), suggest that this number may be too low. Prafull D. Sheth, M. V. Siva Prasada Reddy, Brijesh Regal, Madhulika Laushal, Kaustav Sen, D. B. A. Narayana, "Extent of Spurious (Counterfeit) Medicines in India" (South East Asian FIP-WHO Forum of Pharmaceutical Associations, New Delhi, India, May 31, 2007). A different survey by the Associated Chambers of Commerce and Industry of India found that counterfeit drug sales in the National Capital Region of the country accounted for 20–25 percent of the total medicines sold in the region. The percentage of counterfeits in less well-regulated regions may have been even greater. P. B. Jayakumar, "Asian Nations Unite against Spurious Drugs Trade," *Business Standard*, February 12, 2008, http://www.business-standard.com/common/news_article.php?leftnm=blife&bKeyFlag=BO&autono=313403 (accessed March 17, 2008).

75. India, Ministry of Health, *A Report of the Expert Committee on "A Comprehensive Examination of Drug Regulatory Issues, Including the Problem of Spurious Drugs,"* November 2003, http://cdsco.nic.in/html/ Final%20 Report%20mashelkar.pdf (accessed February 29, 2008).

76. Where the NDPS Act is not enforced, two other parts of the Indian Penal Code can be used: section 120B, which addresses "punishment of criminal conspiracy," and section 420, which addresses confidence tricksters with "punishment for cheating and dishonestly inducing delivery of property." However, there appears to be a reluctance on the part of the Criminal Bureau of Investigations and even the local police to use these parts of the Intellectual Property Code. Few convictions have resulted.

77. In one raid, the CBI urged private intellectual property investigators to gather evidence on premises where Norphine (a morphine derivate injection) was being faked. When one company was raided, yielding R10m ($250,000) worth of drugs but not including Norphine, the CBI could not follow up the case. Vijay Karan (former chief of police, New Delhi, India), personal communication with the author, January 16 and 17, 2008.

78. IndiaLaws, "Narcotic Drugs and Psychotropic Substances (Amendment) Rules," 2007, http://www.indialaws.info/updates/actsrule.aspx (accessed February 28, 2008).

79. *Bangkok Post*, "Editorial: The Scourge of Fake Medicine," February 9, 2008, http://www.bangkokpost.com/090208_News/09Feb2008_news15.php (accessed March 17, 2008).

80. India, Ministry of Health and Family Welfare, *Report of the Expert Committee*.

81. Rajesh Jumar Singh, "Fake Drug Racket in Government Hospitals," *Hindustan Times*, July 28, 2007.

82. Theo Smart, "Revisions to India's Patent Law Could Affect Future Supply of Affordable Generic Antiretrovirals," *NAM Aidsmap News*, March 30, 2005, www.aidsmap.com/en/news/b37b595e-09b6-4499-a93e-9766c0f21ae8.asp?hp=1 (accessed March 17, 2008).

83. D. Roy, "Problem of Spurious/Counterfeit Drugs" (presentation, Central Drugs Standard Control Organization, Ministry of Health and Family Welfare, New Delhi, from the Ministry of Health, Government of India), http://mednet3.who.int/cft/PRESENTATIONS/India (accessed February, 2008).

84. Unnikrishnan, "World Health Organization Says Willing to Help in Fake Drugs Study." According to *India Health News*, the government plans to hire 600 employees, preferably pharmacy graduates, on contract for the project. The employees will be distributed across India's 8,500 talukas (counties) and collect samples from medical stores. *India Health News*, "Health Ministry Set to Launch Campaign against Counterfeit Drugs in February," January 9, 2008.

85. *Hindustan Times*, "Man Sentenced to 15 Years in Jail for Selling Fake Drugs," January 14, 2008, http://www.hindustantimes.com/StoryPage/StoryPage.aspx?id=e6be5aac-f3cd-4f66-8634-80aad5891fec&&Headline=Man+gets+15+yrs+for+selling+fake+drugs (accessed February 8, 2008).

86. *Wall Street Journal LiveMint*, "Central Drug Authority to Be on Lines of U.S. FDA: Ramadoss," January 8, 2008, http://www.livemint.com/2008/01/08115218/Central-Drug-Authority-to-be-o.html (accessed January 22, 2008); *The Hindu*, "India, U.S. to Set Up Food and Drug Authority," January

8, 2008, http://www.hindu.com/2008/01/08/stories/2008010856241300. htm (accessed January 22, 2008).

87. Paul N. Newton, Rose McGready, Facundo Fernandez, Michael D. Green, Manuela Sunjio, Carinne Bruneton, Souly Phanouvong, Pascal Millet, Christopher J. M. Whitty, Ambrose O. Talisuna, Stephane Proux, Eva Maria Christophel, Grace Malenga, Pratap Singhasivanon, Kalifa Bojang, Harparkash Kaur, Kevin Palmer, Nicholas P. J. Day, Brian M. Greenwood, François Nosten, Nicholas J. White, "Manslaughter by Fake Artesunate in Asia—Will Africa Be Next?" *PLoS Medicine* 3, no. 6 (June 13, 2006), http://medicine.plosjournals.org/perlserv/?request=get-document&doi= 10.1371/journal. pmed.0030197 (accessed March 30, 2008).

88. Ibid.

89. For more discussion of the Global ACT Subsidy, see K. J. Arrow, C. B. Panosian, and H. Gelband, *Saving Lives, Buying Time—Economics of Malaria Drugs in an Age of Resistance* (Washington, D.C.: Institute of Medicine, National Academies Press, 2004). For discussion of its benefits and short-comings, see Roger Bate, "Funding Isn't Everything," *American Online*, February 28, 2008, available at http://www.american.com/archive/2008/ february-02-08/funding-isn2019t-everything (accessed March 21, 2008).

90. Primo-Carpenter and McGinnis, "Matrix of Drug Quality Reports in USAID-Assisted Countries."

91. One possible explanation for the ostensible decrease in counterfeiting is the ministry's 2006 announcement that it would amend the Control of Drugs and Cosmetics Regulation of 1984 to make it an offense to possess counterfeit products. Under the existing regulation, individuals selling counterfeit drugs risk being fined up to RM 25,000 ($7,800 U.S.) or jailed for up to three years, and companies face a maximum fine of RM 50,000 ($15,600 U.S.) or three years in jail or both. *New Straits Times* (Malaysia), "Fighting Fakes with New Hologram Labels," December 17, 2006, available with subscription at http://archives.emedia.com.my/bin/main.exe?state= ei90qc.1.1&f=archtoc&p_toc=archtoc&p_search=search&p_help=s_help &a_search=Search&p_s_ALL=Fighting+Fakes+with+New+Hologram+Lab els&p_op_ALL=AND&p_plural=no&p_s_PU=&fdy=2006&tdy=2007&fd m=12&tdm=12&fdd=1&tdd=1&p_L=25&p_SortBy1=DA&p_Ascend1= NO (accessed March 27, 2008).

92. V. Vasudevan, Anis Ibrahim, and Eileen Ng, "Keeping Tabs on Medical Products," *New Straits Times* (Malaysia), September 11, 2007.

93. *Holography News*, "Nigeria Looks to Serialised Holograms," August 1, 2007.

94. U.S. Pharmacopeia, *Ensuring the Quality of Medicines in Low-Income Countries.*

95. The website is at www.buysafedrugs.info (accessed March 17, 2008).

96. Japan Pharmaceutical Manufacturers Association, "International Cooperation Activities," http://www.jpma.or.jp/english/prof/international. html (accessed March 17, 2008), and Japan Pharmaceutical Manufacturers Association, "Panel Discussion at the Scientific Meeting of the Federation of Asian Pharmaceutical Associations," June 18, 2007, http://www.jpma.or.jp/ english/topics/070614.html (accessed March 17, 2008).

97. See note 15 of the introduction.

98. U.S. Pharmacopeia, "About USP—An Overview," www.usp.org/ aboutUSP.

99. Rajendrani Mukhopadhyay, "The Hunt for Counterfeit Medicine," *Analytical Chemistry* 79, no. 7 (2007): 2623–37.

100. More information about the minilab is available at www.gphf.org/ web/en/minilab/index.htm.

101. See chapter 4 for more on track-and-trace technology and RFID.

102. *New York Times*, "Company News: Pfizer Adds Rules Aimed at Stopping Counterfeit Drugs," December 20, 2003, http://query.nytimes. com/gst/fullpage.html?res=9C06E7DE123FF933A15751C1A9659C8B63 &fta=y (accessed March 27, 2008).

103. Nigel Hawkes, "Drug Giant Will Sell Direct to Beat the Counterfeiters," *Times* (London), September 28, 2006, http://www.timesonline.co.uk/ tol/news/uk/health/article652462.ece (accessed March 27, 2008).

104. See the section "Complex Supply Chains Encourage Fakes" in chapter 2.

105. Karan, January 2008.

106. Marci Bough (director of regulatory affairs, American Pharmacies Association), personal communication with the author, October 17, 2007.

107. Scott Gottlieb (former deputy commissioner for medical and scientific affairs, U.S. Food and Drug Administration), personal communication with the author, November 5, 2007.

Chapter 4: Policy Recommendations

1. Roger Bate, "New Malaria Drugs to Be Approved, But Do They Work and Are They Safe?" *TCS Daily*, September 5, 2007, www.aei.org/publication26752 (accessed March 17, 2008).

2. Roger Bate, "Malaria: Poor Drugs for the Poor," *CFD Bulletin*, June 21, 2007, www.aei.org/publication26383 (accessed March 17, 2008).

3. Ibid.

4. For a more extensive discussion of the GPHF minilab, see chapter 3.

5. See chapter 2, note 34.

6. Roger Bate and Kathryn Boateng, "Medicinal Malpractice," *AEI Health Policy Outlook* 10 (December 2006), www.aei.org/publication25276 (accessed March 17, 2008).

7. Roger Bate, Richard Tren, and Jasson Urbach, *Still Taxed to Death: An Analysis of Taxes and Tariffs on Medicines, Vaccines and Medical Devices*, Related Publication 05-04, AEI-Brookings Joint Center for Regulatory Studies, Washington, D.C., April 2005, www.aei-brookings.org/publications/ abstract.php?pid=930 (accessed March 17, 2008).

8. International Policy Network, *Civil Society Report on Intellectual Property, Innovation and Health*, 2006, www.policynetwork.net/main/ content.php?content_id=47 (accessed March 17, 2008).

9. Roger Bate and Kathryn Boateng, "Drug Pricing and Its Discontents," *AEI Health Policy Outlook* 9 (August 2007), www.aei.org/publication26622 (accessed March 17, 2008).

10. Tufts Center for the Study of Drug Development, "Tufts Center for the Study of Drug Development Pegs Cost of a New Prescription Medicine at $802 Million," press release, November 30, 2001, http://csdd.tufts.edu/ NewsEvents/RecentNews.asp?newsid=6 (accessed March 17, 2008).

11. Roger Bate, "Thailand and the Drug Patent Wars," *AEI Health Policy Outlook* 5 (April 2007), www.aei.org/publication25890 (accessed March 17, 2008). In spring 2007, Abbott announced that it would not launch any of its new medicines in Thailand after the country issued compulsory licenses for several frontline drugs.

12. Jayanthi Iyengar, "A Bitter Pill for Indian Drug Industry," *Asia Times* (Hong Kong), December 21, 2002, http://www.atimes.com/atimes/South_ Asia/DL21Df02.html (accessed March 27, 2008).

13. World Trade Organization, "Amendment to the TRIPS Agreement," December 8, 2005, www.wto.org/english/tratop_e/trips_e/wtl641_e.htm (accessed March 17, 2008). According to WTO law, 101 WTO members (or two-thirds of the organization's total membership) must sign the amendment for it to come into official force. As of February 2008, only fourteen countries had done so.

14. Bate, "Thailand and the Drug Patent Wars."

15. U.S. Trade Representative, *2007 Special 301 Report*, 2007, www.ustr.gov/assets/Document_Library/Reports_Publications/2007/2007_ Special_301_Review/asset_upload_file230_11122.pdf (March 17, 2008).

16. U.S. Department of State, "Philippines Improved Intellectual Property Protection, U.S. Says," press release, February 16, 2006, http://usinfo.state.gov/ ei/Archive/2006/Feb/16-97537.html (accessed March 17, 2008).

17. *Davao Today* (Philippines), "US Trade Report Puts Philippines on 'Lower Level Watch List,'" May 2, 2007.

18. Roger Bate, "An Exit Strategy for Big Pharma," *American*, November 27, 2007, www.american.com/archive/2007/november-11-07/an-exit-strategy-for-big-pharma (accessed March 17, 2008).

19. See chapter 2, note 25. Also, Kevin Outterson, "Pharmaceutical Arbitrage: Balancing Access and Innovation in International Prescription Drug Markets," *Yale Journal of Health Policy, Law, and Ethics* 5, no. 1 (2005).

20. Daniel Gilman, "Oy Canada! Trade's Non-Solution to 'The Problem' of U.S. Drug Prices," *American Journal of Law and Medicine* 32 (2006): 247–77.

21. Elvira Draga, "Is Europe Any Closer to a Harmonized P&R Market?" *Global Insight*, November 2, 2007.

22. Panos Kanavos, "The Economic Impact of Pharmaceutical Parallel Trade in Europe," FDA oral testimony on drug re-importation, April 14, 2004, www.hhs.gov/importtaskforce/session3/presentations/Kanavos.ppt (accessed March 21, 2008).

23. London School of Economics, "EU Pharmaceutical Parallel Trade—Benefits to Patients?" press release, January 27, 2004, www.lse.ac.uk/collections/pressAndInformationOffice/newsAndEvents/archives/2004/EU_pharmaceutical_paralleltrade_update.htm. Full report available at Panos Kanavos and Joan Costa-Font, "Pharmaceutical parallel trade in Europe: stakeholder and competition effects," *Economic Policy* (October 2005): 751–98, available at http://www.lse.ac.uk/collections/pressAndInformationOffice/PDF/KanavosHealth.pdf (accessed March 21, 2008).

24. Margaret Kyle, "Strategic Responses to Parallel Trade," Working Paper 12968 (Cambridge, MA: National Bureau of Economic Research, March 2007), www.nber.org/papers/w12968.

25. Pharmaceutical Market Access and Drug Safety Act of 2007, S.242, 110th Cong., 1st session.

26. Bert Moore, "RFID, Bar Codes and Pharmaceutical Authenticity," *AIM Global*, June 7, 2007.

27. U.S. Food and Drug Administration, "Counterfeit Drug Task Force Report: 2006 Update," www.fda.gov/oc/initiatives/counterfeit/report6_06.html (accessed March 17, 2008).

28. Moore, "RFID, Bar Codes and Pharmaceutical Authenticity."

29. Representative Steve Buyer, House Committee on Energy and Commerce, Subcommittee on Health, hearing on HR 3610 (Food and Drug Safety Import Act), 110th Cong., 1st session, 2007, http://energycommerce.house.gov/cmte_mtgs/110-he-hrg.092607.Food.Drug.Import.shtml (accessed March 17, 2008).

30. Ibid.; and Rajendrani Mukhopadhyay, "The Hunt for Counterfeit Medicine," *Analytical Chemistry* 79, no. 7 (2007): 2623–37.

31. EU Heads of Medicines Agencies, "Inspection, Laboratory Control, and Enforcement," Chapter 7 in *Heads of Medicines Agencies Strategy for the European Medicines Regulatory Network*, available at http://www. hma.eu/74.html (accessed March 21, 2008).

32. The FDA's Center for Drug Evaluation and Research estimates that the process takes an average of eight and a half years; the pharmaceutical industry places the number higher, at twelve years. Alliance Pharmaceutical Corp., "Phases of Product Development," www.allp.com/drug_dev.htm (accessed March 17, 2008). Expenditures for OND were $110.6 million in 2005. U.S. Government Accountability Office, *Drug Safety: Improvement Needed in FDA's Postmarket Decision-making and Oversight Process*, GAO-06-402, March 2006, www.gao.gov/new.items/d06402.pdf (accessed March 17, 2008).

33. Ibid. The ODS's task is further complicated by the fact that responsibility for postmarket drug safety is shared among several FDA agencies, often with overlapping or vaguely defined duties, including the Counterfeit Drug Task Force, the Office of Compliance, the Office of Regulatory Affairs, the OND, and the ODS. Unaccompanied by a clear chain of command, the proliferation of agencies with some responsibility for regulating drugs in the market has led to a lack of accountability. Senator Charles Grassley (R-Iowa), speaking on S 1082 (Food and Drug Administration Revitalization Act) and HR 2900 (Food and Drug Administration Amendments Act of 2007), on July 26, 2007, to the full Senate, 110th Cong., 1st session, *Congressional Record* 153: S.10136.

34. U.S. Food and Drug Administration, "Notice of Public Meeting," 2007N-0005, January 16, 2007, www.fda.gov/OHRMS/DOCKETS/98fr/07n-0005-nm00001.pdf (accessed March 17, 2008).

35. Randall W. Lutter (congressional testimony, Subcommittee on Criminal Justice, Drug Policy, and Human Resources, Committee on Government Reform, U.S. House of Representatives, November 1, 2005).

36. Ibid.

37. National Association of Boards of Pharmacy, "Model Rules for the Licensure of Wholesale Distributors," June 19, 2006, www.nabp.net/ftpfiles/NABP01/WholesalerModelRules.pdf (accessed March 17, 2008).

38. Mark Thornton, *The Economics of Prohibition* (Salt Lake City: University of Utah Press, 1991); and Michael 't Sas-Rolfes, *Rhinos: Conservation Economics and Trade-Offs* (London: IEA Press, 1995).

39. Roger Bate, "Fake!" *American*, September/October 2007, http://american.com/archive/2007/september-october-magazine-contents/counterfeits-kill (accessed March 17, 2008).

40. Roger Bate and Kathryn Boateng, "Bad Medicine in the Market," *AEI Health Policy Outlook* 8 (2007), www.aei.org/publication26368 (accessed March 17, 2008).

41. See chapter 3, note 11.

42. James C. McAllister III, "Counterfeit Drugs and the 'Secondary Market,'" *Pharmacy Times*, 2003.

43. Bate, "An Exit Strategy for Big Pharma."

44. See chapter 2, note 25.

45. Lamphone Syhakhang, Solveig Freudenthal, Goran Tomson, and Rolf Wahlstrom, "Knowledge and Perceptions of Drug Quality among Drug Sellers and Consumers in Lao PDR," *Health Policy and Planning* 19, no. 6 (2004): 391–401.

46. Armina Ligaya, "Counterfeit Drugs Caused Woman's Death, Coroner Concludes," *Globe and Mail*, July 6, 2007. Also discussed in chapter 2, "How and Why Does Counterfeiting Occur?"

47. See the NABP's VIPPS website at http://www.nabp.net/index.html?target=/vipps/intro.asp&.

48. Royal Pharmaceutical Society of Great Britain, "News Release: Millions Risk Health Buying Drugs Online," January 10, 2008, http://www.rpsgb.org/pdfs/pr080110.pdf (accessed March 27, 2008).

49. World Health Organization, International Medical Products Anti-Counterfeiting Taskforce, "Meeting Conclusions" (IMPACT Technology Sub-Group Meeting, Prague, March 13, 2007), www.who.int/impact/activities/IMPACTmeeting_conclusions.pdf (accessed March 17, 2008).

About the Author

Roger Bate is a resident fellow at the American Enterprise Institute. He researches aid policy in Africa and the developing world, evaluating the performance and effectiveness of the United States Agency for International Development, the World Bank, the Millennium Challenge Corporation, NGOs, and other aid organizations and development policy initiatives. He writes extensively on topics such as endemic diseases in developing countries (malaria, HIV/AIDS); access and innovation in pharmaceuticals; taxes and tariffs; water policy; and international health agreements. Mr. Bate's writings have appeared in the *Lancet,* the *British Medical Journal,* the *Journal of the Royal Society of Medicine,* the *Wall Street Journal,* and the *Financial Times,* among other pubications. In the process of writing *Making a Killing,* Mr. Bate conducted extensive research in India and numerous African countries.